Diary of an American Exorcist

Stephen J. Rossetti

Diary of an American Exorcist

Demons, Possession, and the Modern-Day Battle against Ancient Evil

SOPHIA INSTITUTE PRESS
Manchester, New Hampshire

Nihil obstat: Reverend Monsignor Charles E. Pope, Censor Deputatus
Imprimatur: Very Reverend Daniel B. Carson, Vicar General
and Moderator of the Curia
Archdiocese of Washington, March 16, 2021

The *nihil obstat* and *imprimatur* are official declarations that a book or pamphlet is free of doctrinal or moral error. There is no implication that those who have granted the *nihil obstat* or the *imprimatur* agree with the content, opinions, or statements expressed therein.

Sophia Institute Press
Box 5284, Manchester, NH 03108
1-800-888-9344

www.SophiaInstitute.com

Sophia Institute Press® is a registered trademark of Sophia Institute.

hardcover ISBN 978-1-64413-467-2

ebook ISBN 978-1-64413-468-9

Library of Congress Control Number: 2021934651

Fourth printing

Contents

A Prayer for You

May the Blessed Virgin spread her mantle of protection over all who read this book, or any part of it, with their loves ones and all they possess. May St. Michael and the holy angels establish a perimeter of protection around you all. May the blood of Christ wash you clean of any evil. May the light of Christ shine through you so brightly that it casts out every darkness. I pray especially that the love, joy, and peace of Christ fill your hearts in this world and the next. Amen.

A Note of Gratitude

I am grateful to many people. I think of our graced and terrific exorcism team members. They are very gifted, dedicated, and faith-filled. It is a grace for me to minister alongside them.

I am grateful for our many prayer warriors scattered around the globe. Your quiet prayers and sacrifices are critical to the success of this ministry.

I am grateful to the Archdiocese of Washington for its unwavering and generous support of our healing ministry.

I am grateful to our many generous donors who make our healing ministry possible.

Diary of an American Exorcist

Introduction

I am often asked how I became an exorcist. The answer is quite simple: the Blessed Virgin picked me.

The journey started with a powerful spiritual experience when I was a seminarian. One night, I had just gone to bed but hadn't fallen asleep yet. Suddenly I was invisibly attacked. It was unbelievably powerful and incredibly fast. With a graced insight, I instantly knew what it was. Satan was attacking me. And I was going to be quickly overwhelmed.

My rosary beads were on the table at the foot of my bed. The moment the attack started, I instantly thought of these beads. I lunged out of bed and thrust out my hand to grab my rosary. The instant I touched the beads, the attack stopped. So I went back to bed and fell quickly asleep.[1]

---

[1] How did I fall asleep so quickly? My first thought is, "I was tired!" But more concretely, intense spiritual experiences often carry with them a special grace to understand and interpret them. I knew exactly what happened: I was attacked by one of Satan's demons, and the Blessed Virgin Mary cast him out. I knew I was in the good hands of a loving Mother. So I slept like a child in his mother's arms.

3

In those two seconds, I learned about 80 percent of what an exorcist needs to know. Satan is very powerful and moves at lightning speed. Angels, and demons, travel at the speed of thought. I am no match for Satan; even the smallest of demons is exponentially stronger than any human. But the Blessed Virgin casts out the prince of darkness and his minions with ease. If I hold on to her, I will be safe and she will protect me. And when it's all over, I can go back to sleep and be at peace.

Twenty-five years later, I was appointed a diocesan exorcist. I have been one now for over a dozen years. Our little exorcism team has a *very* active caseload. We receive many new calls each week, plus we handle dozens of ongoing cases. So there have been lots of experiences to fuel these diaries! And wherever I go, my rosary beads are *always* on my person. Even when I sleep, these beads are wrapped around my left hand.

The diary entries are not exaggerated in any way. Some details of individuals have been altered or deleted to protect the individuals' identities. But each of the entries is a factual account of my daily experiences or the experiences of our team. They are the truth, without varnish or hype. You may believe them or not. But they are what we exorcists experience and talk about among ourselves. When I speak to other exorcists around the country and in other countries, I find that my experiences are very similar to theirs. There is a common body of exorcism knowledge that is growing, based on our common experiences.

After a number of the diary entries, I have included "theological reflections." These are meant to explain in more detail some of the theological truths and realities presupposed in these diary entries. The reflections often include citations from the Scriptures and insights of Church Fathers and other theologians. I hope they will help you to understand the entries more fully.

Nevertheless, much of the world of angels and demons remains a mystery to us.

Despite all the demonic antics and the havoc that Satan can cause, it is my hope that the underlying message will come through: there is only one God and one Savior, Jesus Christ. When faced with the infinite power of God, Satan is a "dust bunny." His actions are limited, and his time is very short. Soon, he will be cast into the pit forever.

In the meantime, we trust in God, hold fast to the salvation of Jesus, and invoke the protection of the Blessed Virgin, the saints, and the angels. We have no reason to fear. I sleep very well at night (despite the occasional demonic attacks!).

Be at peace. Jesus has already won the battle.

Exorcist Diary 1

"Stop Saying That Name!"

In the middle of an exorcism session, out of the mouth of the energumen (a possessed person) came the cry "Stop saying that name!" We had been saying the holy name of Jesus, and it was really getting to the demons. They hated to hear it. So, realizing they hated it, we said it all the more. Again and again, we chanted, "Jesus, Jesus, Jesus."

The name of Jesus is holy. It should never be used in vain or as a cuss word. This would be like throwing something holy in the mud. "At the name of Jesus every knee should bend, of those in heaven and on earth and under the earth" (Phil. 2:10). I often quote this passage in the midst of a session and emphasize the phrase "under the earth." Even in Hell, the name of Jesus is all powerful, and every knee should bend.

On earth, the name of Jesus has power to cast out demons. As the Rite of Exorcism says, *"In nomine Domini nostri Iesu Christi eradicare et effugare ab hoc plasmate Dei"* which is, "In the name of our Lord Jesus Christ: be uprooted and be put to flight from this creature of God."

How many saints have died with the name of Jesus on their lips! But to the demons, His name is torture or, truly, a pure Hell.

Invoking the Name of Jesus

In the time of Jesus, as well as in our own day, doing an action "in the name of" someone meant doing it on that person's behalf. One is delegated to act in that person's stead with all the requisite authority and power. Since we are one in Jesus, it is Jesus Himself who acts through us when we do His will. We read in Colossians: "Whatever you do, in word or deed, do everything in the name of the Lord Jesus, giving thanks to God the Father through him" (Col. 3:17).

This is true of casting out demons as well. The exorcist has no authority over demons except that which the Lord Himself gives through the delegation of the bishop. Jesus explicitly told us to act on His behalf to cast out demons. We read in the Gospel of Luke: "He summoned the Twelve and gave them power and authority over all demons" (Luke 9:1). When the demons hear the exorcist invoke the name of Jesus, they are directly confronted with the power and authority of Jesus Himself. Against Him, they are no match.

Exorcist Diary 2

Dropped Call or Demons?

A priest in need of consultation tried to call me this morning. He had a thorny case of someone who, he believed, had a real demonic problem. As I would find out later, he had just used his cell phone in that same spot a few minutes earlier and it had worked fine. At that time, I was also at a good spot with good reception. All other calls that day went through fine. But this priest and I tried to call each other at least a dozen times. We would begin to speak, and then the line would immediately go dead.

Something was afoot. After many dropped calls, I got the priest on the phone again, and before we were disconnected, I quickly said, "Let's say a prayer." We prayed to the Blessed Virgin Mary and St. Michael, asking for their intercession to keep the phone lines open. Our prayers were answered. No dropped call that time. We had a good chat. And it turned out that he really did have someone who was in strong need of deliverance from demons.

Quite often, I find that possessed people will have great problems connecting on the phone to their pastor, spiritual director, or exorcist. I've heard from many of the people I have helped over the years that they often cannot get through to me on the phone.

We see a clear pattern of demonic interference in trying to stop these troubled people from getting help. The demons do whatever they can to isolate their targets. Staying in touch with a priest is the last thing the demons want. And, believe it or not, demons love to mess with gadgets!

Solution? Pray over the phone lines to keep them clear.[2] Also, we typically have a backup way to stay in touch as well. We may use Skype or some other app. Sometimes there are disruptions this way too. So we may contact a close friend or family member who then contacts the afflicted person on our behalf. It is more an annoyance than anything else. We eventually find a way to get through to the person in need.

The demons can slow us down. But with a little perseverance and prayer, we get through. This is typical of demonic harassment. They can stall, harass, and try to make things difficult, but in the end, God always triumphs!

---

[2] See the app Catholic Exorcism at the St. Michael Center for Spiritual Renewal. Under "Deliverance Prayers for the Laity" is the "Umbrellino Prayer for Technology," https://www .catholicexorcism.org/deliverance-prayers-for-the-laity.

Theological Reflection

What Is Demonic Possession?

Demons are fallen angels. And, like all angels (and humans too), they were created to be in a loving unity with creation, with one another, and with God. We were all built for relationships. Unfortunately, the fallen angels, or demons, as they are called, rejected God and thus rejected all that God is.

God is first and foremost a loving Trinitarian relationship of Father, Son, and Holy Spirit. God's loving Trinitarian union is offered to all of us, which is fully realized in the life of Heaven.

Because of their radical sin, demons cannot build and enter into such loving relationships. There are no friendships in Hell. The demons' primal urge for union remains, but it is now distorted, and instead of engaging in free, loving relationships, demons try to control, dominate, and possess.

This is true of dysfunctional, distorted human relationships as well. Human beings are called to free, loving relationships with others. But, as a result of sin, some human relationships are characterized by attempts to control and possess. This is not of God.

When given an opening, demons will therefore try to enter and possess. They can possess an object, such as a cursed occult artifact. They can also possess a place, especially if sinful or occult behavior has occurred there.

A house, an apartment, or another building can be "infested" with demons if someone invites them in, even unknowingly. Or sometimes it can be a person who has an "open door" to the demonic.

Oftentimes the demonic possession remains hidden. But there are times when the demons' presence becomes manifest. For example, a possessed person who undergoes a conversion and starts practicing the Faith may begin to manifest the possession. Going into a church, praying, or any such religious practice can be the occasion for hidden demons to react strongly in the possessed person's body. Possessed people can have great difficulty entering a church. They may struggle to recite prayers. When sprinkled with cold holy water, they may say that it burns. Or they may avert their eyes from a crucifix or a holy painting. This is all because of the presence of demons, who cannot stand such holy objects or prayers.

In cases of full possession, at times the demons will take over complete control of the person's body. The demonic personality may even manifest on the person's face. The person's voice will change, and it will no longer be the human person speaking but the demons. In such cases, the demons are controlling the person's body, and thus the person becomes what is called "possessed" by demons.

Exorcist Diary 3

Strong versus Weak Possession

In our first session with someone who is suffering and asking for help, we try to determine whether the person is possessed or just oppressed or suffering from a psychological problem, or both. This is primarily a discernment. Part of the discernment is to pray over the person and see if there is a reaction to the prayers we recite.

The demons cannot stand the prayers of the Church and eventually react violently if they are present in an individual. The best analogy I can think of is to imagine pouring boiling, flammable oil over the demons and then lighting it afire. That's how God's grace and holy objects feel to them; they scream in agony. Since they are not mortal, they cannot die. But they are *very* strong, and so they sit there and scream while they are being burned alive yet still do not leave immediately.

In a recent discernment, we prayed over a young woman who we thought might be possessed. As we began to pray, she thrashed and screamed. She reacted violently to holy water and a crucifix as well as St. Benedict medals. The pure hatred in her eyes, and especially hatred of us priests, was very diagnostic. This is one strong sign of a demonic presence and one that human beings cannot imitate. It is unnerving.

The client was psychologically normal with no real signs of psychological deficits. Her father, we found out, engaged in some occult behavior when she was young and appeared to have involved her in some way. He was sheepish about it and reticent to admit such things to his pastor.

Sadly, we determined after some time that she was possessed. But her possession was somewhat "weaker," a lesser possession, if you will. The demons moved from arrogance and defiance in the beginning of the session to whining and crying fairly quickly. Moreover, when I commanded them to do something, they responded. At the end of the session, I asked the person what she remembered and she said, "Everything." This is a typical sign of a weaker possession.

When the possession is strong, the client goes "out" quickly, often during the initial Litany of the Saints. The eyes roll back, and the person loses consciousness. Then the demons manifest. They are usually arrogant, diss the priests, and refuse to do anything I tell them. They tend not to show any strong reaction to the sacramentals or prayers, at least in the beginning sessions.

But in a weaker possession, as in this case, the demons start to whine and cry fairly quickly. As already noted, the person remains aware of what happens during the session, although the individual's consciousness is still in the background. It is the demons' personalities that come to the forefront when they manifest in the session. The demons, in these cases, are obedient and forced to do what I ask, such as kissing the cross and keeping their arms down and not hitting others. And they react strongly to blessed holy objects.

So, this possession was weaker, perhaps because the afflicted person herself did not do anything wrong to warrant possession. It was likely something her father did. Moreover, she has been living a good Christian life and engaging in a strong sacramental life too. This means the demons' grip is usually lighter and it takes less time to eject them.

As we have continued to pray over this person, she has made wonderful progress. She is quickly getting her life back. This is a joy to see. This ministry has been very encouraging and rewarding for me.

What Is Demons' Manifesting?

If a person is possessed, the demons are able to take over the person's body for a period of time and manifest, or reveal, their presence. The exorcist looks for signs of a demonic manifestation to make the diagnosis of a true possession.

A possessed person can manifest a demonic presence anytime. A demonic manifestation is more likely to happen when the person is engaged in holy, religious activities such as going to a church service, praying, or, especially, undergoing an exorcism. Normally, the demons try to hide their presence. During an exorcism or any holy activity, however, the demons suffer greatly and have difficulty hiding.

Because the demons have willingly given themselves over to evil, they cannot stand what is holy or good. They have rejected the One who is infinitely good and now cannot be in the presence of what is of God. Putting them in the presence of anything good is akin to making someone who lives in the darkness stare directly into the light of the sun. So, when the light of goodness shines on them, they react or manifest.

There are many typical signs of a demonic manifestation, and these can vary from person to person. Some of the classic signs include writhing and showing an aversion to holy objects. In more serious cases, the demonic presence will temporarily take over the personality of the afflicted person, and the person's consciousness will recede into the background. Then the demons can speak through the person's voice and the look on the person's face will often reflect a demonic rage. In such instances, the demons are fully manifesting, and it is clear that the person is possessed.

Exorcist Diary 4

Facing Lucifer

The team and I spend a lot of time dealing with lower-ranking demons. Most people who are possessed have such lesser demons. Thank God. If we get their names during the exorcism, they are not commonly known.

Occasionally we run into a higher-ranking demon, and then it gets rougher. These are the more well-known princes of Hell, such as Beelzebul, Baal, Leviathan, Gressil, and Asmodeus. There are moments when Lucifer himself shows up. These are rare. Some demons who inhabit the possessed claim to be Satan or Lucifer but are usually lower-ranking demons perhaps under their direct command. When Lucifer shows up, he is typically surrounded by Hell's princes and many, many others. This is ugly.

During a recent session, I was interrogating the demons and commanded them to tell me who was the leader of the possessing demons. The demonic spokesman answered with an arrogant sneer, "The King of Hell himself is our leader." He added, "You're way out of your league." Later they confirmed that it was Lucifer himself. Ugh.

We had been exorcising this person for a year and a half, and after all the lower demons had been cast out in Jesus' name, including Hell's princes, Lucifer himself finally came to the fore. His personality was unique and unmistakable. He came forward with a hiss that sounded like a snake. He was not like the lower demons, who were often superficially boastful, adolescent, and shallow. Despite their innate intelligence, they acted quite stupidly.

Lucifer, whose name is often translated as "Light Bearer" or "Morning Star" (Isa. 14:12), was brilliant, cunning, measured, and deadly. Lower demons cower in the presence of a priest, but Lucifer did not. Later, I consulted an older exorcist, who said, "They are trying to intimidate you to see if there is any lack of confidence in you, which they will pursue." He added, "Don't take the bait."

It would be a tough spiritual battle, but the team and I had to trust. Lucifer had a *very* strong army. He marshaled all of his considerable resources, including the princes of Hell and hundreds of demons. But we had the power of Heaven: the Blessed Virgin Mary, the saints and angels, and, of course, Jesus Himself. We couldn't lose.

I invoked the Blessed Virgin Mary and prayed the Church's official Rite of Exorcism, with our lay team praying the litanies. The "King of Hell" screamed and writhed like all the rest. As the ancient Rite of Exorcism itself says, "*Cede igitur, cede non mihi, sed ministro Christi,*" that is, "Yield, therefore, yield, not to myself but to the minister of Christ." Eventually, as with all the others, the power of Christ cast him out.

The Highest Angel Fell

The following passage from Isaiah is often applied to Lucifer, "How you have fallen from the heavens, O Morning Star, son of the dawn! How you have been cut down to the earth, you who conquered nations!" (14:12). The Vulgate translates "Morning Star" as "Lucifer," which a number of Church Fathers identified as Satan.[3]

Lucifer's sin, according to St. Thomas Aquinas, was seeking to be as God, by his own nature rather than by God's grace. Thus, Lucifer sinned through pride.[4] Others identify the sin of Lucifer as one of envy.

There are also conflicting opinions as to whether Lucifer was the highest angel before the Fall. St. Thomas agrees with Pope St. Gregory the Great that Lucifer (or Satan) was indeed the highest angel.[5] I would add that the difference between the lower angels and the higher angels is not simply one of a modest degree but an exponential step up in power and intelligence. As the highest angel, Lucifer must have been surpassingly brilliant! Sadly, he must have been blinded by his own brilliance.

[3] Raymond E. Brown et al., *Jerome Biblical Commentary* (Englewood Cliffs, NJ: Prentice-Hall, 1968), 274.
[4] St. Thomas Aquinas, *Summa Theologica* (ST), I, q. 63, arts. 3, 7.
[5] *ST*, I, q. 63, art. 7.

Lucifer has great disdain for human beings. By nature, he is so much greater than we puny humans are. What Jesus, the God-Man, is by nature, however, we humans can become by grace. What we can become through grace far surpasses even the angels. By sharing in the divine nature of Jesus, we are raised up, by grace, to participate in God's very being (Heb. 1:5).

This is astounding. In the beginning, the angels knew of the eventual Incarnation of the Son of God. He was to become human—not an angel. It is believed that Satan rejected this divine act of humility and God's love for humans.

Satan wars against all humans to spite God the Father and to spite the Son. Similarly, we humans conquer Satan, despite his innate superiority, precisely through our participation in Jesus. In Jesus, we share in the divine nature and we cast out Satan in His name.

Exorcist Diary 5

Why Do Demons Choke People?

A man recently called and said his house was infested with demons. He added that they attacked him in bed and choked him. He had difficulty breathing. But he instinctively managed to sputter, "In the name of Jesus, get off me!" He said this three times. Finally, the demons stopped.

Many people who are attacked by demons say that they are sometimes choked by them. In the midst of exorcism sessions, the possessed person will not uncommonly start choking. During one of the most difficult cases we have had, the demons said to me, through the mouth of the possessed person, that they were "forced" to choke this person because of what the exorcism team was doing to them. So the demons tried to blame it on me. My response was a sardonic "Nice try."

Demons do bad things. They do not take responsibility for their bad behavior. And they try to make us feel guilty.

Why do demons choke people? First, it is something animals do. They grab their prey by the throat to subdue it and to kill it. Demons are not allowed to kill people, but they can choke people in certain limited circumstances, especially the possessed (Job 1:12; 2:6).

Demons act like vicious beasts and are often depicted in art as animals or figures with animal attributes such as tails, claws, and horns. They choke people to try to establish their authority over them and to frighten and intimidate them. They also choke them to stop them from praying or speaking the name of Jesus. If you've ever been choked, you know how terrifying it can be.

But, rest assured, God does not allow the demons to kill us. Also, the proper response to demonic attacks is to do what the man being choked spontaneously did: he commanded the demons, in Jesus' name, to stop. We all have authority over our own bodies, and we can exercise this authority by telling the demons to leave us.

Demons try to establish their control through intimidation and fear, like a pack of wild beasts. They are full of empty bluster and hollow threats. We should remember always that Jesus is Lord! Trust in Him.

Theological Reflection

Satan on a Short Leash

It is common for exorcists to speak of Satan as being on a short leash. Satan's actions are not the work of God. God never seeks to tempt us to sin or to harm us. But God allows Satan some limited measure of freedom to tempt and harass. This begs the question: Why would God allow such a thing to happen?

One answer is this: God allows the devil some free rein so that we might grow in grace and holiness. I often witness this. Those whom we pray over typically are strengthened in their faith and become committed to living holy lives, completely free from Satan's grasp. Ironically, even the evil actions of Satan ultimately promote God's will and redound to the glory of God, to Satan's eternal rage.

Satan and the demons are purely spiritual beings. They exist outside of the physical reality that we humans experience. As previously noted, they are much more powerful than we are, and they move with the speed of thought. We are no match for them, by ourselves. Thus, their actions must be greatly limited. We are never tempted beyond our strength. Demons are limited in the harm they can cause in the world. Otherwise, Satan would kill us all and the world would be destroyed in fire.

With their limited freedom, demons cannot directly kill or maim us. But they can and do try to frighten and dominate us. As noted earlier, demons act like beasts, and in cases of possession and severe oppression, they can cause pain. They can choke people. In one horrible case, the demons choked a person repeatedly. She "greyed out" numerous times, although she never completely blacked out. It was an incredible trial for her and for those who witnessed such brutality.

No doubt, for many, such brutal behavior does not seem fair, and people question God's allowing such awful things. This is part of a much larger question: Why does God allow suffering in the world? Why did God allow the holocaust, the black plague, COVID-19, widespread famines, and many other scourges? We will ultimately find out when, hopefully, we are in the presence of God in the next life. For now, we trust in God and believe that "all things work for good for those who love God" (Rom. 8:28).

Exorcist Diary 6

Upping Your Game

I was recently giving a training session for new exorcists. A few were a little skittish, fearing demonic retaliation. I assured them the ministry was safe. God would protect them. But I did add, "You need to up your game." I explained. Being an exorcist is like flying an airplane (I used to be in the Air Force). It is very safe … but mistakes can be deadly.

First, there is no such thing as a "little" sin. Any sin is awful. It is also a fissure that Satan can drive a wedge into. Do you have a problem with alcohol? Sexuality? Pornography? Disobedience? Arrogance? Self-hatred? Anger? Clean up your act first, and then come back.

The *prenotanda* (introduction to the Rite of Exorcism, no. 13) advises that the ministry "is to be granted only to a Priest endowed with piety, knowledge, prudence and integrity of life." I stress the last part: integrity of life. Satan will have a field day with someone who is not living priesthood with integrity.

Moreover, the exorcist should work diligently and carefully to conform his life to Christ and His Church. We exorcist priests typically go to Confession weekly, say the Divine Office with devotion, do more than one daily holy hour, and are scrupulously obedient to our superiors and to the Church. Satan will use the slightest crack in our spiritual lives to get into our heads and wreak havoc.

But there is one trait above all that is essential; perhaps it is the only trait that really matters: trust. The exorcist must trust in the power of Jesus Christ, no matter how dark things look. Jesus is Lord!

We sleep well at night because Jesus is Lord. We walk into every session with confidence because Jesus is Lord. There is no doubt in our minds how this will all end because Jesus is Lord.

It is a beautiful ministry. Jesus is Lord.

Exorcist Diary 7

Attacked by Demons

Rough case today. The team and I thought it would be a simple case of a mild demonic oppression. As we began the prayers of liberation over a middle-aged man, I was attacked by his demons. My stomach became instantly nauseated, and the ill feeling quickly spread to my head and the rest of my body. My whole being felt spiritually pummeled throughout the session. It was difficult to stay in the room and continue the session. Ugh.

After the session was over, a gifted person in the room (before I could tell him my experience), said he saw the demons attacking me when we started to pray. He also described precisely what I had experienced: they first attacked my stomach and then went to my head. Gifted people, or spiritual sensitives, have a God-given charism that helps them to discern spiritual realities, often including the presence of demons (see the theological reflection "Spiritual Sensitives" on page 53).

I took his words as a confirmation that I am not crazy! All of us in this ministry need to be careful in discerning what is real and what is imagined. Being pummeled by demons is an experience that is hard to mistake.

As strange as it may sound, this attack was also a grace. Now we know that this person has a serious demonic problem. So we will schedule many more sessions. And I hope and pray that, as the demons attack us, it is a grace for the afflicted person and more quickly results in his liberation. Praise the Lord!

Can Humans Be Attacked by Demons?

There is a long history of people being attacked by demons, especially the great saints. We call this Satan's "extraordinary" activity. His "ordinary" activity against all humanity is to tempt us to sin. But sometimes Satan is allowed to attack people directly. It is important to note that this is not common.

Many saints have reported being physically beaten up by demons. God allows this for the sanctification of the saint and also as a participation in the Cross of Jesus. As the afflicted person willingly accepts the attacks and overcomes them with God's grace, it can become a source of grace for many others. This is because these sufferings are offered in union with the one sacrifice of Jesus Christ.

Possessed people, too, are not uncommonly the subject of extraordinary demonic attacks. Demons are allowed to attack possessed people in a variety of ways. For example, possessed people sometimes have unexplained scratches and bruises. In fact, we have seen such scratches and bruises appear on the body of a possessed person in the midst of a session. Demons can afflict possessed people in many other direct, and very distressing, ways. As noted previously, it is not uncommon that demons will choke possessed people.

St. Thomas Aquinas speaks of these demonic temptations and attacks when he writes, "The wicked angels assail men ... by instigating them to sin, and thus they are not sent by God to assail us, but are sometimes permitted to do so according to God's just judgments.... In order that the conditions of the fight be not unequal, there is for man the promised recompense, to be gained principally through the grace of God, and secondarily through the guardianship of the angels."[6]

As mentioned earlier, demons are inherently more powerful than human beings in their nature. Thus, God restricts what demons can do and gives human beings the necessary graces and protection to overcome demonic harassment. Those attacked by Satan should trust in God and pray for deliverance, confident that in God these attacks will be overcome.

[6] *ST*, I, q. 114, art. 1.

Exorcist Diary 8

Plumber or Holy Water Needed

I remember one very difficult exorcism case. The demons present were high-ranking and thus very powerful. It was a long and terrible battle.

At one point during the 1½-year process, one of the assisting priests was having problems in his rectory. The plumbing was plugged up, and the toilets didn't work. It lasted for more than a week. He had plumbers in on several occasions, and they could find nothing wrong. They assured him that his waste system was fine. But why wasn't it working?

He mentioned the problem to me, and recognizing that his problem might not be physical, I responded, "Try throwing some holy water on it." He did, and everything immediately started working again.

Demons love to harass us. God typically does not allow them to hurt us seriously, so they do whatever they can to tempt, frighten, harass, and intimidate. As I tell the team, do not be swayed by such adolescent tricks. Jesus is Lord! Trust in Him.

But it does go to show you: sometimes in life you need a plumber, but other times, you need a bit of holy water.

Theological Reflection

Demons Try to Dominate and Possess in This World

Angels and demons are everywhere. We do not know their exact number, but we know it is *very* large. St. Thomas said, "Hence it must be said the angels ... exist in exceeding great number, far beyond all material multitude."[7] He also suggested, "More angels stood firm than sinned."[8]

Some theologians speculate that one-third of the angels fell and became demons, applying the book of Revelation: "It was a huge red dragon ... its tail swept away a third of the stars in the sky and hurled them down to the earth" (12:3–4). The Italian priest and mystic Padre Pio (1887–1968) said, "There are so many [demons] that if they were capable of assuming a form as tiny as a grain of sand, they would block out the sun."[9]

Holy angels, on the other hand, have a mission to protect and guide according to God's will. They do not try to possess or dominate. They are instruments of God's love, and thus they enhance our freedom. Demons are

[7] *ST*, I, q. 50, art. 3.
[8] *ST*, I, q. 63. art. 9.
[9] See Associazione Amici di Carlo Acutis, "Saint Pio of Pietrelcina," Real Presence Eucharistic Education and Adoration Association, http://www.thereal presence.org/eucharst/misc/Angels_Demons/ANGES _pietralcina.pdf.

out to possess, to control, to dominate, and ultimately to destroy. Thus, demons try to infest places and establish dominion, all for their evil purposes.

If given an opening, either through human sin or human invitation, the demons are able to possess people and places. For example, people who engage in occult behavior give Satan an invitation, and he will try to possess and dominate. Moreover, in places where sinful or occult behavior has occurred, demons try to attach themselves to a place and claim it as their own. Thus, they infest houses and dominate areas as well. Many so-called haunted houses are actually infested with demons.

So, when a spiritual sensitive "sees" a demon on a person, in a place, or on a cursed object, it means the demon was able to assert some sort of bond and control, either by sinful behavior or direct invitation. The count-less numbers of demons would like nothing better than to control people, things, and places in God's creation.

For a limited time, Satan and his demons are allowed to wreak some havoc on this material world. But when the end-time comes, they will be cast permanently into Hell, and their influence will be limited to the confines of Hell.

Exorcist Diary 9

The Grace of Discernment

A wise old exorcist once told me, "Pray for the gift of discernment to do this ministry. You'll need it." Discernment is a daily task for an exorcist.

Again today, I sifted through many requests. A woman said she recently had a "recovered memory" that she was ritually abused by Satanists at the age of two and is now possessed by Satan. She complained about her three previous exorcists who tried to help, and she said they all failed. Hmmm. This is possible, but three exorcists failed? No, we won't take this case.

A middle-aged woman complained that she was possessed by demons that were put into her by public officials, but she couldn't complain to the police because they were "in" on it. Paranoid. Again, no.

Then I received an e-mail, full of loose associations and bizarre reasoning, in which the person claimed possession by a demon. Major thought disorder. No.

But one caught my eye. The person sounded fairly sane. She had a long list of unexplained illnesses. She tried many doctors, and none of them knew what was wrong. She had recently come back to the practice of her Faith. Previously she had been involved in the occult but eventually realized her mistake. Now, when she tries to receive Communion, she gets ill. She finds it increasingly difficult even to walk into a church. Hmmm. Maybe.

This last one bears a closer look: a possible case of oppression, perhaps even possession. We will ask for much background information, subject the person to a psychologist's eye, and then set up an appointment, to include praying over her. We will note how she reacts to the prayers. We shall see.

I feel bad turning away many desperate people. But they likely don't need an exorcism, despite their protestations. I remember another experienced exorcist saying, "If someone tells you categorically that he is possessed, he is probably not. But if he acts truly surprised at his bizarre symptoms, he just might be."

God grant me the wisdom to discern and the grace to help and to heal where I can.

Exorcist Diary 10

Whom Are You Dialing?

A woman came to us in a panic. She initially was involved with Reiki, a universalist energy therapy condemned by the United States Conference of Catholic Bishops (USCCB).[10] Later, her beloved father died, so she tried to contact him through automatic writing. She was left-handed, so she put a pen in her right hand and invoked the spirit of her deceased father. The pen started to move, and over the course of several months, she received many loving and consoling messages from her deceased father, or so she thought.

Then the messages started to go south. They became ugly and threatening. She started to realize that this entire time it was not her loving father with whom she was in contact. Rather, it was an evil spirit. She was terrified!

We had her immediately stop this necromancy (summoning the dead) and sacramentally confess this sin. She formally renounced this practice, and we prayed deliverance prayers over her. Fortunately, the evil spirit receded and apparently did not return.

---

[10] Committee on Doctrine, United States Conference of Catholic Bishops, "Guidelines for Evaluating Reiki as an Alternative Therapy," USCCB, March 25, 2009, https://www.usccb.org /resources/evaluation-guidelines-finaltext-2009-03_0.pdf.

People often ask me about many non-Christian spiritual practices: yoga, Reiki, ancestor worship, Ouija boards, Charlie Charlie, white witchcraft, and the like. "What do you think?" they ask me. The answer is simple: if you are not calling on the one true God and Jesus, His Son (or the Blessed Virgin Mary, the saints, or St. Michael and the good angels), then there is only one other spiritual option, and that is Satan.

Do Demons Beat Up Other Demons?

Yesterday, we were in the process of exorcising the last demon out of a person, by the grace of God. While manifesting, the person (demon) looked up and got a worried look. I commanded the demon to tell me why it was not leaving. It said, "The others will beat me up. They are calling me a coward." Clearly, the demon was frightened.

This reminds me of a case we had a few years ago. As the demons were weakening, they could not resist and were forced to start answering my questions. When demons start being obedient to the exorcist, we know they are weakening and close to leaving.

As I pumped the demons for helpful information on how many demons were left, the names of the leaders, and other pertinent info, the demons tried to stop answering. When I demanded to know why, the leader said, "The others will beat me up. They are already angry that I gave this information."

Some mystics have had visions of Hell and noted that demons beat up the humans in Hell. It's massively ugly. But demons beat each other up too. Demons maintain their strict angelic hierarchy in Hell and demand slavish subservience from lower-ranking demons. They do so by threats and beatings, even among their own kind. Don't believe it? Nevertheless, this has been our experience in exorcisms.

Hell is not a democracy. It is a place of slavish torture and violence. It is all that the demons know; it is who they are.

Theological Reflection

The Demonic Hierarchy

St. Thomas writes that angels are not equal in intelligence and power, but rather are divided into nine choirs, existing in a natural hierarchy of greater and lesser.[11] Though the exact delineation of those choirs may differ slightly among authors, St. Thomas, citing the authority of Scripture, lists them from highest to lowest: seraphim, cherubim, thrones, dominations, virtues, powers, principalities, archangels, and angels.[12]

After the fall of Satan and his minions, the demons retained their natural hierarchy, with higher-ranking demons having greater natural intelligence and power than the lower demons. Our experience in trying to exorcise higher-ranking demons versus lower-ranking ones is that the power differential is exceedingly great. Lower-ranking demons are much easier to exorcise. When one runs into a higher-ranking one, it is exponentially harder to cast it out.

In Hell, there is a kind of order based not upon love and unity, as in Heaven, but upon domination, fear, and evil. St. Thomas noted, "Demons are not equal in nature, and so among them there exists a natural precedence."[13] In addition, he said, "demons are by

---

[11] *ST*, I, q. 108, art. 3, reply obj. 1.
[12] *ST*, I, q. 108, art. 5.
[13] *ST*, I, q. 109, art. 2, reply obj. 3.

natural order subject to others; and hence their actions are subject to the action of those above them."[14]

Because of the demons' wickedness, narcissism, and consuming hatred, authority is exercised in Hell in the most brutal of fashions. It is self-serving, harsh, and sadistic.

Ironically, the demons refused to be obedient to their loving Creator, which would have given them true freedom. Rather, they ended up as slaves to higher-ranking demons and ultimately to Satan. They ended up, as Jesus warned, "slaves to sin" (John 8:34).

---

[14] *ST*, I, q. 109, art. 2.

Exorcist Diary 12

Slimed by Demons

After a few minutes of praying, the demons manifested. They were wagging a finger at me and shaking the energumen's head. I had been commanding the demons to leave and the response was pretty clear: "No!"

Then came a mocking, evil smile over the person's face. If there was any doubt that this woman was possessed, it was gone. The look conveyed incredible arrogance and a complete disdain. There was no kindness, no mercy, no sensitivity—just contempt. I felt ridiculed and "slimed."

So I walked up to her, looked her in the eye, put a crucifix six inches from her face, and repeated the ancient formula: "*Ecce crucem Domini; fugite partes adversae*" (Behold the Cross of the Lord; take flight you hostile powers), and then I sprinkled holy water over her. Her body reacted violently. In an exorcism, the demons are engulfed in a holy torture that we believe is worse than the fires of Hell. They were writhing in pain.

It's called spiritual warfare and appropriately so. Recently, an afflicted person went through a similar intense session, and he was exhausted for three days after it. He asked why. I responded, "This is normal, especially in the beginning. An exorcism is an intense struggle, and it is spiritually exhausting."

But eventually the demons weaken. The sessions become less intense. The afflicted person gets spiritually stronger. The arrogance of the demons disappears, and finally the demons leave with a whimper.

At the end of each session, we do a "cleansing" prayer. We pray that the Blood of Christ would wash us clean of any evil that may have attached to us. We need that spiritual "shower." The demonic arrogance and slime are ugly. But they are always washed away by God's grace.

Exorcist Diary 13

Round Two

In a very rough case, an individual was initially infested with almost nine hundred demons, a fact that the demons revealed only under duress. After praying for over a year, the number slowly started to dwindle, which gave us all much hope.

At one point, we finished a session, and the count was down to 704. At the beginning of the following session, however, I demanded to know how many were present, and they said, "Seven hundred twenty." I repeated it, "Seven hundred twenty? I thought it was 704." The response came with a gloating, almost jubilant sneer, "Round two." Rats. The demons had been reinforced.

Thus, the demons indirectly admitted they had lost "round one," and the demonic colony was crumbling. Once the entire demonic colony in the afflicted person gets weak enough due to hours of exorcistic praying, the demons start to leave rather quickly.

So they called in reinforcements. It turns out that the leader of this new group was Gressil, a well-known, powerful demon. But after a few sessions, Gressil and his group were expelled. Round two for Jesus!

Recently, we had a case in which we were down to two leading demons and their followers. Then all of a sudden, one of our gifted team members, who can literally see demons, noticed that a third demon arrived on the scene. "Where did he come from?" I asked. She just shrugged her shoulders.

Reinforcements. Ugh.

So we spiritually pounded away for a long time, and it finally left. I spent the rest of the day in bed, spiritually exhausted. Our gifted team member, too, was wiped out for three days. No doubt about it, demons suck the energy out of us. We paid a spiritual price to expel the demonic reinforcements, but it was worth it.

A demonic colony in a person can be reinforced. There are certainly plenty of demons in Hell to go around. But, fortunately, the Lord doesn't allow this to happen too often. We exorcists say the Umbréllino prayer (see the theological reflection below) at the beginning of each session to surround the demons with the good angels and to stop any reinforcements. It usually works. But sometimes they are allowed to call in backup anyway.

Although it is bad when this happens, the good news is that reinforcements typically have less of a hold on the person and are more easily exorcised.

Theological Reflection

The Umbrellino Prayer

At the beginning of each exorcism session, to prevent Satan from reinforcing the demons present in a person, an exorcist typically recites the Umbrellino, or "umbrella," prayer. This prayer asks Almighty God to "establish a perimeter of protection" around the afflicted person and around the entire team, "where Satan and any other evil spirit … cannot empower or aid in any way, the demons present here, rendering deaf, dumb and blind, unable to communicate or receive any empowerment from any other evil spirit by isolating them from each other."

The exorcist also asks God's grace in "destroying any ability of these to fortify their stronghold, lengthen their stay, or strengthen their ability to attack or hide." Thus, the exorcist prays that the demons in the afflicted person would be isolated and not able to receive any support from Satan or any other demons. Of course, God is free to grant this request or not, depending on the divine plan.

We have had exorcism sessions in which the afflicted person claimed to see other demons in the room. We have also had the demons in the afflicted person call out to other demons and ask for help. At such moments, we have one of the priests present exorcise the room, while we continue to exorcise the individual. Thus, he casts out any demons who are "hanging around."

Exorcist Diary 14

Don't Eat a Demon

I was having lunch with one of our gifted laity, a spiritual sensitive. We are blessed in having several. This person has the gift of seeing demons. The server placed the plates of food in front of us, but my companion did not start eating. It was a noticeably awkward moment. Finally, she looked up and said, "Aren't you going to bless the food?"

By her demeanor, I knew something was up. I answered, "Is there something wrong with the food?" She nodded but said nothing. I guessed, "Are there demons on the food?" She said quietly, "Yes."

I gave the typical blessing over a meal. She said the demons quickly left. Again, when the dessert came out, she hesitated. So, I asked again, "Are there demons on this too?" Again, she said softly, "Yes." This time I made her say the blessing and these demons left too.

It kind of makes you wonder what was going on in the kitchen! This was a rare occurrence (as far as I know) that this person saw demons on food. I wonder if one of the kitchen staff was cursing the food before it was brought to the dining room. This might seem odd, but I have found out that there are more people cursing things and engaged in occult practices than I would have expected.

If we had eaten the food with the demons on it, I don't know for sure what would have happened. No doubt it wouldn't have been pleasant. I probably would have chalked it all up to indigestion or something.

The moral of the story: don't go anywhere without your own mystic! Ha! Also, you can bet I am a bit more diligent about blessing meals before I eat them. Who wants to eat a demon?

Theological Reflection

Spiritual Sensitives

The core of an exorcism is a priest with faculties praying the Church's official Rite of Exorcism. Thus, it is the Church praying, with all her authority given by Christ, which is wielded by the priest. Against Christ and His Church, the demons are defenseless.

Exorcists, however, often rely on the gifts of "spiritual sensitives" or "gifted" people to assist them. These people have charisms or gifts given by God that are often very helpful to exorcists. Some theologians, such as Alois Wiesinger, O.C.S.O., in *Occult Phenomena*, say that, before the Original Sin of Adam and Eve, human beings naturally had a plethora of preternatural gifts, such as seeing angels and demons. After the Fall, some human beings have retained remnants of these abilities.

There are many kinds of such preternatural gifts, but we exorcists especially appreciate someone who can sense the presence of demons and even the kinds of demons present. For example, in one session, a gifted priest sensed the presence of an evil spirit of death. This was conveyed to the exorcist, who then prayed out loud, commanding the demons of death to leave the afflicted person.

Specifically identifying the demons gives the exorcist a bit more power over them and helps to exorcise them more quickly. In this case, the person did have a history of suicidal attempts and the demons of death did depart. As a result of the session and the specific prayers casting out the demons of death, the afflicted person experienced considerable relief.

Knocked Off Center

It was another ugly session today. The demons manifested and were nasty and very evil. Should I have expected anything else?

Here is one way to know that the person is really possessed: you look into the face of the afflicted person who is in the throes of manifesting a demon and you don't see the person. Rather, it is pure evil staring back at you. This is a bit unnerving.

I came home after this session and felt "off center." I didn't feel right inside. My peace was gone, and I felt like crying. I wanted to curl up in the corner or maybe take a big drink. But those human "remedies" don't help. They can't cure the toxicity of evil.

I went into the chapel and gave my problem to God. Things weren't right inside, and I gave that to God. I vowed to pray for my usual time in the afternoon, about thirty minutes. So, I sat there. Slowly, the peace came back. I was again centered, and my heart was at rest.

This experience helps greatly with diagnosis. The woman in today's session is clearly possessed. Facing the demons disturbs one's inner peace of heart. Only God can bring the inner peace back.

Being an exorcist means looking into the eyes of evil — often. It is unsettling. But God takes care of me. God is there at the end of the day when I need to be put back together.

Theological Reflection

Experiencing the Demons' Hell

Jesus promised His disciples: "Peace I leave with you; my peace I give to you. Not as the world gives do I give it to you" (John 14:27). One of the great gifts of being a follower of Jesus is that divine inner peace that Jesus gives. We are brought into a right relationship with God, others, and self. Thus, we experience a deep sense of inner peace.

This peace does not exist in Hell. Rejecting God and Jesus results in a lack of inner peace. Hell is, rather, a place of perpetual unrest and dis-ease. There can be no true happiness and no inner peace for anyone who rejects God. Perhaps this is one reason there is so much violence and unrest in the world today.

To look into the eyes of evil and to be close enough to experience its "Hell" is unnerving. Love is replaced by hatred. Unity and peace are replaced by discord and violence. Feeling that complete hatred and violence is upsetting. It rightly disturbs one's soul.

There is nothing glamorous about an exorcism. It is an ugly affair in which the powers of Hell are exposed. At times, those in the room get a taste of the demons' Hell. Fortunately, in the end, Jesus overcomes, and His peace prevails.

Exorcist Diary 16

Silly Gilly Gumbo

There are a number of cases reported where dogs (and cats) are able to sense the presence of demons. I think some of them can see demons. In the book *The Demon of Brownsville Road*, the family dog parked himself next to the couple's bed at night to protect them and barked when the demons approached.

One of our spiritual sensitives who sees demons has a dog that also senses the presence of demons. The dog will bark when demons are approaching, usually a few moments before the demons are in sight of the person. So the dog provides her with a little warning, although she says that the dog is "worthless" in getting rid of them. Apparently, demons are not afraid of dogs and pretty much ignore them.

Some very young children can also see demons. A priest told me about a man who had rented a house to an older gentleman. Unfortunately, the renter was summoning the dead with a Ouija board—a big no-no! The famous movie *The Exorcist* is based on the story of a young boy who used a Ouija board for months and became possessed. Surely the man's house is now infested with demons.

As the man came out of the house holding the Ouija board, his little girl told her mother that Daddy was coming out of the house followed by a "silly gilly gumbo." The mother knew what the girl meant and blanched. No doubt, it was a demon.

When we get older, we lose the childlike simplicity and a child's occasional ability to see the spiritual—angels and demons.

Doors for the Demonic

When discerning whether a person is possessed, the exorcist will scrutinize the individual's history, looking for any doorways through which demons could have entered. There are many types of doorways.

One obvious type is conducting occult activity. This could involve summoning the dead, witchcraft, spells or curses, pagan rituals, Ouija boards, seances, voodoo, Santeria, or other pagan or demonic spiritualisms. Making an explicit pact with Satan or being dedicated to Satan is especially disastrous.

There are other kinds of doorways including committing serious sins. Having a history of drug or alcohol abuse or other addictions can be a doorway. A significant history of sinful sexual activity may also result in a demonic presence. We have noted the devastating impact of abortion, especially when family members are regularly engaged in conducting abortions. Any sort of serious sin is an invitation to Satan.

People can also become possessed through no fault of their own. Childhood traumas can be gateways to a demonic presence. We have seen a number of people who appear to have become the subject of demonic activity by being cursed by another person. Curses seem to be especially effective if the person sending the curse is a practicing occult member or even a member of one's own family with authority over the cursed individual, such as a mother or a father.

All of these are possible doorways that allow Satan and his demons to enter a person's life. Sometimes people become possessed because of these actions. Other times, they might experience a lesser impact, such as demonic oppression. Despite having open doorways, some people may dodge the bullet and not be the subject of Satan's extraordinary activity at all. Yet these activities will likely have a deleterious effect of some sort on the individuals involved. In the end, it is a mystery why some people become possessed and others do not, given similar circumstances.

Exorcist Diary 17

You Stupid Priest!

One thing an exorcist learns quickly is that demons *hate* priests! During one intense session, the possessed person, in the midst of a demonic manifestation, looked at me with rage and disgust and said of my client, "I hate the day she met you!"

A diagnostic moment often occurs when the person whom we are praying over looks at the priest with an evil and angry look and says, "You stupid priest!" If I had a dollar for every time I heard that, we could fund our ministry forever. It's one of their most often repeated lines. When we hear it, it confirms our diagnosis that the person is indeed possessed.

We believe that the priest is sacramentally configured to Christ. So, when the demons look at the priest, it is really the face of Christ they are seeing. This causes them unbelievable torment.

When the demons get particularly snarky and look at me with disgust, I will often say, "I command you that when you look at me, you will see the face of Christ." This command wipes the snarky look off their faces, and they cower in fear. Sometimes they start to whimper and cry. Demons are cowards and are nothing in the presence of Jesus.

Can Laypeople Exorcise Demons?

The Catholic Church's canon law stipulates that only a priest expressly delegated by the local bishop can con- duct a major exorcism on a possessed person (canon 1172). So, if a person is truly possessed, then this min- istry is reserved for a delegated priest.

A major exorcism of a possessed person is complex and often difficult. Moreover, it can be spiritually dan- gerous if not conducted properly. It requires training and supervised experience. By analogy, one would not want heart surgery to be done by someone who is not a trained and experienced surgeon. Moreover, the priest has a special sacramental protection and functions *in persona Christi capitis* (in the person of Christ the head) in his ministry, which makes it spiritually safer and typi- cally more fruitful.

In the history of the Church, there have been reli- gious and laypeople with a special charism to cast out demons, usually based on their great holiness. St. Cath- erine of Siena (1347–1380) was sometimes asked by the local priests to exorcise a possessed person when they could not. She was very successful at casting out demons, as were a number of other particularly holy and gifted saints.

Most people with demonic problems are not fully possessed and do not need a major exorcism. They may be experiencing demonic oppressions, obsessions, or harassment that might benefit from what are called deliverance prayers or a minor exorcism. Anyone can validly pray deliverance prayers, particularly those who are baptized Christians. They can appeal to the power of God in Jesus to cast out demons. However, for their own spiritual safety, it is recommended that they be in a state of grace and spiritually prepared and selected for such a ministry.

Also, it is commonly recommended to the laity that they not address demons directly or use "imperative" prayers that directly command demons to leave. Rather, they should direct their deliverance prayers to God, Jesus, or the Mother of God or the saints and angels. These are called "deprecatory" prayers. There have been cases in which laypeople have gotten in over their heads spiritually in confronting demons directly. So the Church's limitation on who can perform a major exorcism is for the safety of all. Some caution in conducting deliverance prayers or minor exorcisms is warranted as well.

Exorcist Diary 18

Living with the Angels

Our exorcism ministry can be viewed as a work of the angels. The archangel Michael and legions of angels cast Lucifer and his reprobate angels out of Heaven. We continue their work on this earth. We are fortunate to be allowed to share in this angelic work. Thus, we should be "breathing the air" of the angels.

We exorcists are ministering among the angels and are surrounded by them. A mystic told me that at every exorcism there is at least one angel from the rank of powers present and helping. At more difficult exorcisms, we have had as many as eight in the room with us.

To "breathe the air" of angels, we need to detach a bit more from worldly values and live more intentionally in their spiritual realm. Eventually, as our life is more consciously lived in the company of angels, they become our companions and friends. We are living in good company and it is a joy!

Theological Reflection

St. Michael and the Angelic Powers

The Catholic Church takes the words of the book of Revelation quite literally regarding the battle between St. Michael and the angels and Lucifer and his demons: "Then war broke out in heaven; Michael and his angels battled against the dragon. The dragon and its angels fought back, but they did not prevail.... The huge dragon, the ancient serpent, who is called the Devil and Satan, who deceived the whole world, was thrown down to earth, and its angels were thrown down with it" (Rev. 12:7–9).

Jesus' death and Resurrection has definitively defeated and destroyed Satan's kingdom. But the spiritual battle for souls continues to rage on this earth, and St. Michael and the angels continue to wage war with Satan on our behalf. The angels are especially present during an exorcism, which is a clear moment of spiritual warfare.

Of the nine choirs of angels, it is thought that the rank of powers is particularly present in exorcisms. These angelic powers are of a higher rank than that of the guardian angels and thus have greater power in assisting in the casting out of demons.

St. Michael, as protector of the people and the leader of the angelic host that cast out Lucifer, continues to lead the angelic host in repelling Satan's attacks, especially in an exorcism. In religious iconography, St. Michael is usually depicted with sword in hand and Satan under his foot. Exorcists, naturally, have a close affinity to St. Michael and often invoke his help.

Exorcist Diary 19

Exorcising Judas

At a recent conference for exorcists, I was talking about a difficult exorcism that lasted almost two years. At one point in the exorcism session, an evil personality came forward and said, out of the possessed person's mouth, that its name was Judas. I commanded to know whether it was a demon using the name or really was the person of Judas, who betrayed Jesus. He shouted, with a tinge of shame, that he was the human person.

Though some exorcists debate whether fallen souls can inhabit a possessed person, others have told me that they, too, have encountered Judas, the fallen disciple. Although it is not an article of faith, the Bible gives one the impression that Judas is indeed in Hell.

During the conference, I recalled how difficult it was to cast out Judas. Other high-ranking demons were exorcised more easily. It seemed that Judas was impervious to the Rite of Exorcism, holy water, and just about everything else we tried. Finally, according to the other demons upon interrogation, Mary herself came and cast out Judas. Why did we have such difficulty with a lowly human being when we were able to cast out powerful demons in Jesus' name?

One of the other participants said his team had the same problem with Judas. But they realized that Jesus gave His disciples His authority to cast out demons but not to cast out fallen human beings. This made sense. We simply had no authority over Judas. He was not a demon. Fortunately, the Mother of Jesus came and cast him out herself. She knew we needed her help!

At the conference, it was striking how similar were the experiences of exorcists in different places on this point and on many others. We all found the commonality of our experiences to be very affirming. There is a concrete, objective, demonic reality out there, and we are all facing it.

Exorcist Diary 20

Demons Hate Hell

Demons want to hang on to their possessed people. Time and again during an exorcism, they whine and say they don't want to leave. It reminds me of the demons named Legion mentioned in the Bible who begged Jesus, as He was exorcising them, to let them go into the swine (Mark 5:1–20). Apparently, they don't want to go back to Hell, a truly horrifying place, made worse by their own evil misdeeds.

In the course of an exorcism, it is often difficult to get rid of demons. They cling tenaciously. In one session, when I was trying to exorcise a demon, it stubbornly resisted, saying, "I like it here."

Demons will try every trick in the book to stay. They will hide and make you think they are gone. They will try to keep the possessed person from coming to the sessions. In the sessions themselves, they will beg and plead, or, conversely, they will act as if they are unfazed by it all. One of their favorite lines is "We will never leave." But they do.

Eventually, demons act like desperate beasts facing their own destruction. They flail and scream. I can still hear Lucifer himself when he was personally cast out by the Virgin Mary. He screamed, "Noooooooo" three times. And then he was gone.

Lucifer and his minions themselves have helped to make hell the horror that it is. It is an unspeakably awful place. The demons do everything they can to avoid going back.

The Sufferings of Hell

There are many today who deny the existence of Hell or minimize its horrible torture. Jesus is repeatedly clear about the reality and description of Hell: "Depart from me, all you evildoers! And there will be wailing and grinding of teeth when you see Abraham, Isaac, and Jacob and all the prophets in the kingdom of God and you yourselves cast out" (Luke 13:27–28; see also Matt. 8:12).

St. Faustina, a great Catholic mystic and religious, was given a vision of Hell. She said, "Most of the souls there [in Hell] are those who disbelieved that there is a hell."[15]

She described the seven tortures of Hell, starting from the worst: (1) loss of the vision of God, (2) the perpetual remorse of conscience, (3) the realization that this existence will never change, (4) an internal spiritual fire, (5) continual darkness, a horrid smell, and the sight of demons and other damned souls, (6) the sight and presence of Satan, and (7) despair, hatred of God, and continual blasphemies. Sr. Faustina added, "I am writing this at the command of God, so that no soul

---

[15] *Diary of Saint Maria Faustina Kowalska: Divine Mercy in My Soul* (Stockbridge, MA: Marian Press, 2005), no. 741.

may find an excuse by saying there is no hell, or that nobody has ever been there."[16]

As we will read in a later diary entry, Hell is actually a mercy. Damned souls and fallen angels could not endure the presence of infinite holiness, blazing light, and eternal glory, which is Heaven.

An exorcist sees this very clearly in each session; the mere sight of a holy object such as a crucifix or a drop of holy water gives the demons excruciating pain. What would it be like for them to see God directly? This would be the cruelest of tortures for the fallen and the damned. Sadly, it is a Hell of their own choosing.

[16] Ibid.

Exorcist Diary 21

Ugly but Blessed

A couple of days ago, I received an interesting text from one of our team members after she assisted at an exorcism session. She said she felt graced during the session. She texted, "It was like being inside a warm house during a storm."

Exorcisms are indeed stormy. The possessed often scream. Many of them vomit. So, we try to have a waste basket with a plastic bag at the ready.

Both of these actions, screaming and vomiting, are actually good signs. If the person screams during the session, it means that the prayers are very effective and the demons are writhing in pain as God's grace touches them. When the person begins to throw up, it is typically a sign that some of the demons are starting to leave.

Despite all of this ugliness, team members often tell me they walk out of a session feeling graced. God's grace touches them in a quiet but palpable way. I must say, it is the same for me. An exorcism is an ugly, ugly event. Though I walk out of a session feeling drained, there is also a deep sense of God's peace.

Theological Reflection

The Blessings of an Exorcism

Many people are frightened of the exorcism ministry, even some priests. I spoke to a priest yesterday who said the whole idea of it frightens him, and he refuses to talk about it. People have told me that even thinking about it gives them nightmares. On the other hand, there are some who are inordinately fascinated by evil. The latter is no better than the former and is maybe even worse.

If one is called to this ministry, it is a great grace. To those who are called, God will give the right gifts. One of those gifts is a bit of fearlessness in the face of evil. The person might even be given the righteous spirit of St. Michael, who is incensed at the outrageous actions of demons and marshals his angels in battle to throw them out.

Moreover, we have found that each exorcism session, despite the nauseating evil presence and ugly demonic antics, carries with it a grace for all the faithful present. As a symbol of this and as an instrument of this grace, I typically lay my hands in blessing on each of the faithful at some point during the session.

God is never outdone in generosity. Would God be less generous to His disciples when continuing Jesus' exorcism ministry?

Nevertheless, Jesus taught His disciples a balanced perspective. After being sent out by Jesus to evangelize, "the seventy-two returned rejoicing, and said, 'Lord, even the demons are subject to us because of your name.'" Likely, they were surprised and exhilarated that they were able to cast out demons using Jesus' name. Then the Lord said, "Nevertheless, do not rejoice because the spirits are subject to you, but rejoice because your names are written in heaven" (Luke 10:17, 20). Exorcizing demons is good, but most important is our salvation in Christ.

Exorcist Diary 22

Where Are the Demons?

In the midst of a recent prayer session, the demons had fully manifested and were controlling the possessed person's body. At the beginning of the session, I had placed a St. Benedict medal (about 1¾ inches in diameter) in each of the person's hands, as I often do. (When manifesting, the demons may complain that these blessed objects burn them.)

The demons that possess a person are attached to particular points on the body. The locations are sometimes based on the sin or doorway that allowed them to enter—for example, on the hands if the person has engaged in sinful behavior with his hands.

I commanded the demons to tell me how many they were, and the response was "three." I then commanded them to put a St. Benedict medal where one of the demons was. The person's right hand went to the left side of her chest. I commanded the demons to put a medal on the next location, and it went on the person's throat. Then I commanded them to put a medal on the third spot, and it was on the forehead.

I laid my hand with the priest's stole on the woman's throat, and the demons went nuts. The woman choked and doubled over. It was clearly a strong reaction, and this demon was losing it. It appeared that it finally left. The woman confirmed afterward that she thought something left from her throat area.

I've never commanded demons to locate themselves before, but it seemed to work. I am cautious because they are inveterate liars. In the past, I have asked our charismatic people to locate the demons, and we concentrated on those places. This is a new tactic that might work in other cases, but only if the demons are weak enough to be obedient.[17]

---

[17] I did this again today with another possessed person, and again the hand with the medallion went to the left side of the chest. When we prayed specifically over this spot, the demons howled! This tactic can definitely work!

Theological Reflection

Sacramentals

The Catholic Church teaches that there are seven sacraments, which have been instituted by Jesus and give us grace for our salvation. They are Baptism, Confirmation, Eucharist, Penance (Confession), Anointing of the Sick, Marriage, and Holy Orders. These are the normal road to growing in faith and holiness and thus finding salvation in Christ.

With her own authority, given by Christ, the Church has instituted special sacramentals. These do not give sanctifying grace like the sacraments but rather offer actual graces to help us live out our sacraments more fully. Sacramentals find their efficacy in the intercession of the Church.[18] They help sanctify the daily moments of our lives.

As the *Catechism of the Catholic Church* teaches, first among the sacramentals are blessings of people, meals, places, and objects.[19] The Rite of Exorcism itself is also a sacramental.[20]

Common sacramentals used in the Rite of Exorcism are a crucifix and holy water. Another sacramental is the Benedictine medal. It is one of the only sacramentals that has an exorcistic formula written on it.

---

[18] *Catechism of the Catholic Church* (CCC), no. 1667.
[19] CCC, no. 1671.
[20] CCC, no. 1673.

On the outside rim on the back of the Benedictine medal are the letters: VRSNSMV-SMQLIVB. The meaning of these letters was unknown for some time, until an explanation was discovered in a manuscript dating to 1415, found in the Abbey of Metten in Bavaria. These stand for the Latin exorcistic formula: *Vade retro, Satana! Nunquam suade mihi vana! Sunt mala quae libas. Ipse venena bibas!* This means: "Begone, Satan! Never tempt me with your vanities! What you offer me is evil. Drink the poison yourself!"[21]

[21] "The Medal of Saint Benedict," OSB.org, https://www.osb.org/the-medal-of-saint-benedict/.

Exorcist Diary 23

Anger Feeds the Demons

I learned, again, how toxic anger can be. I was in the midst of an exorcism session, and the energumen leapt up and attacked me. That has happened before, but it is unusual. Normally there is a kind of spiritual bubble around me; God does not usually let the demons physically attack me during a session. However, I typically get a lot of verbal abuse from the demons in many sessions, and they certainly try to get into my head.

Fortunately, the possessed person who attacked me was not physically strong, being rather petite. But it took a couple of team members to contain her. No doubt some demonic strength was in her. I got angry when she attacked me, and I gripped her arm tightly, although I didn't show the anger on the outside. Nonetheless, the demon's voice chided me for losing my temper. (They never miss an opportunity to diss me!)

Sure enough, as we continued the session, the demons stopped reacting and seemed unfazed by the whole thing. Something was wrong. I stopped the session, went into the other room with one of the priests, and confessed the sin of losing my temper. The other priest absolved me, and we went back into the session. Once again, the demons started to react to the prayers.

The demons were feeding off my anger. *A good note to self*: confess any unhealed anger before entering a session; also, try not to let the demons provoke you. When you get angry, then they have a hook in you, and the sessions stall out.

Exorcist Diary 24

Snake Eyes

Sometimes it is difficult to determine whether a person is possessed or whether his or her problem is psychological only. Other times, the truth is obvious.

In one case, while the demons were manifesting, even the appearance of the person's eyes changed: they became yellow with small black pupils and looked exactly like the eyes of a snake. In other cases, someone's eyeballs will turn completely black.

In the book of Genesis, Satan is portrayed as a serpent that tricks Eve into eating of the forbidden fruit—that is, into sinning. In the past, some have thought of a snake as merely a metaphor for Satan. But the serpentine eyes of this possessed man suggest that a snake is more than a distant image of the demonic. During an exorcism, Satan himself came forward with a deep hiss and sounded like a snake. I will never forget his voice.

Demons are very real, and they are akin to an evil, cunning, slithering animal. At times, demons even look and sound like an evil snake-like creature, especially Satan himself.

Theological Reflection

Unusual Demonic Manifestations

The usual demonic manifestations are these: the person thrashes in response to holy objects and prayers, the person displays hidden knowledge of team members or events, and a demonic personality comes forward in the midst of a session and speaks at the exorcist, usually in derogatory words.

Demons will sometimes manifest their presence by moving objects, turning electronic devices on and off, creating the sound of pounding footsteps, manifesting orbs of light or flashes of light, or slamming windows and doors. They manipulate physical objects in an attempt to intimidate and coerce.

But there are less-typical forms of manifestation, such as in the case above where the normal human eyes of the afflicted person were visibly transformed into the eyes of a snake. We have seen objects materialize out of nothing, including drug paraphernalia and bottles of alcohol in the case of addicts, presumably as a temptation or torture for the afflicted person.

Other exorcists have shown us photos of a variety of objects that were ejected from orifices of the afflicted during an exorcism, including nails, spikes, hair, small figurines, a large chain, and voodoo dolls. In one case, the person, rather grotesquely, expelled a huge snake.

Another exorcist team informed us that one of their afflicted persons levitated during a session.

Demons cannot perform miracles. Only God can perform miracles or empower others to do so. But demons can do what is "natural" for them. This includes superhuman strength and knowledge of hidden events, as well as levitating, materializing, or manipulating objects. So, what seems miraculous to us when demons are acting is really just natural for them.

Exorcist Diary 25

Riling Satan

A new exorcist recently asked me if he would likely experience some retaliation from Satan in the course of his ministry. Another experienced exorcist and I guffawed. I said, "Of course. You can't stick a knife in Satan's eye day after day and not expect him to get a little riled." The new exorcist blanched, "I thought we were protected!" Well, yes, we are protected from serious harm, but that doesn't mean a demon won't do everything that God allows him to do. This will likely include a bit of harassment.

One of our priest exorcists, in the midst of a big case, woke up one morning with long scratches on his arm. It was clear where they came from. We have had a variety of demonic harassment through the years, but never anything life threatening—although I do remember walking down the stairs at 3:00 a.m. during that same case and having my legs fly out from under me. Now I always make the Sign of the Cross before walking down the stairs late at night.

Should we stop doing this ministry so we don't rile Satan? Nonsense. Jesus is Lord! We follow Him and do His will. If Satan is angry with what we do, that's good. We are not here on earth to make Satan happy (which is impossible anyway). In fact, if in your entire life you have not made Satan angry and have never been the target of his wrath, are you really a Christian?

Exorcist Diary 26

Demon Brain

I was sitting and calmly interviewing a woman whom we thought might be possessed. She is a practicing Christian and was speaking rationally and was clearly a believer. However, she was concerned, as was her priest, at her strange manifestations during prayer and especially when the priests prayed over her. Sadly, as a child, her parents had been heavily involved in witchcraft and other occult practices. They had offered their daughter to these evil spirits.

As I was speaking to her, she suddenly changed her attitude completely. She looked fine, but what came out of her mouth stunned me. She said, "Satan will defeat you. You will never get rid of these demons. They are too strong for you." I started to argue and to explain that Jesus defeated Satan on the Cross and it was in His name that the demons would be cast out.

But the client wasn't budging. "You have no authority. It is useless." The other exorcist looked at me and said quietly, "Demon brain." "Of course," I thought, "How could I be so stupid?" It was no good arguing with her because I was really talking to a pack of demons. Instead, I went back to praying and commanded, "*Exorcizo te, Satanas!*" (I exorcise you, Satan!)

When demons get into people's heads, especially possessed people, the people might look normal, but they start thinking like demons; they have "demon brain," as we call it. I'll bet there are more than a few people we meet during the day whose minds are filled with demons. Listen to what comes out of people's mouths. Is it a rational human being speaking or an angry, God-hating, arrogant demon?

Theological Reflection

A Parent's Authority

Having a God-given authority over demons is important for casting them out. The priest exorcist is especially empowered to conduct a solemn exorcism. But any baptized Christian has some authority to cast out demons. Recall the previously cited Scripture: "The seventy-two returned rejoicing, and said, 'Lord, even the demons are subject to us because of your name'" (Luke 10:17). So baptized Christians can invoke the name of Jesus to cast out demons, although the Church has reserved solemn exorcisms for the exorcist. Deliverance prayers for lesser demonic presences, however, are suitable for laypeople.

As noted in the theological reflection "Can Laypeople Exorcise Demons?" (see entry 17), the laity should not address demons directly but should rather address God or the Blessed Virgin Mary or saints and angels to drive out the demons. Thus, in most cases, in their deliverance prayers they do not use "imprecatory" prayers commanding the demons, but rather "deprecatory" prayers that beseech God's help. If the individual begins to manifest in marked ways suggesting a possible possession or at least a strong oppression, the person should be referred to a priest.

There are times when the laity do have a special authority to cast out demons. For example, parents have a God-given authority to pray over and bless their children.

Thus, as an exception to the previous rule, *parents can command demons to leave their children*. Nevertheless, I think it wise for parents to seek expert assistance before doing so. In the case of a true possession, it would also be wise to enlist a priest with such faculties. But in situations where there are no priests with training or faculties available, this might indeed warrant strong measures. Moreover, if a child begins unexpectedly to manifest a demonic presence, a parent might step in and invoke a parent's authority over the demons.

This same parental authority over children also empowers parents' blessing over their children. Scripture teaches us that parents have the authority to bless their children (for example, see Genesis 27 and Isaac's blessing his son). Unfortunately, this tradition has been lost among many families, and children are the worse for it. The parents' blessing should be rediscovered and used liberally.

It is appropriate for parents to bless their children on a variety of occasions, such as when they're going to bed at night, when they're going on a trip, and for special events such as an engagement or any other significant moment. The blessing of a parent is a unique grace for children, whether it is to sanctify a particular moment in their lives or to rid them of an evil presence.

Isolation and Demons

One of our possessed clients seems a bit stuck. I inquired about her personal life, and it turns out she is very isolated. She has no friends and stays by herself. I asked her why, and she said that she can't make any friends. "No one will understand my situation," she remarked. In recent weeks, I have asked a few of our afflicted souls about their relationships, and several have echoed the same isolation.

Demons themselves are isolated. There are no friendships in Hell. Possessing demons work hard at keeping their victims isolated, thus making the possessed in their own image. If the possessed stay isolated and without the life-giving consolation and grace of true friendships, can they ever be truly liberated?

It is the demons who whisper in their ears that no one will want to be their friends; no one will understand them. This is another characteristic of "demon brain." The isolation of the possessed allows the demons greater control over their victims.

To be liberated, the possessed need to embrace the person of Jesus, who is the source of all true liberation. And they need to return to the community of the faithful—not only worshipping with others but also enjoying the nurturing life-giving relationships within this community. Living a life of isolation feeds the demons.

Was Peter Possessed?

A few years ago, I was listening to one of the best demonologists and exorcists in the United States privately speculate that St. Peter might initially have been possessed. I must admit that I was *highly* skeptical. It is true that the Gospels record Jesus looking at Peter and saying, "Get behind me, Satan!" (Matt. 16:23). We often use this line in exorcisms: *Vade retro, Satanas!*

But it would mean that Jesus intentionally picked a possessed person to be one of His closest disciples. It is hard to believe. But I remind myself that one of Jesus' closest followers was Mary of Magdala, out of whom He cast seven demons.

Stories of exorcists often seem exaggerated and somewhat fantastical to those outside of this ministry. No doubt many of my recollections in this diary might seem so to those unfamiliar with this often bizarre world. Nevertheless, I myself was very doubtful of the speculation that Peter had been possessed.

But a short while ago, we were in the midst of an exorcism, and one of the priest exorcists pulled out a relic of St. Peter and applied it to the body of the possessed, whereupon out of the mouth of the possessed person came a mocking voice, "He used to be ours!" I spontaneously responded, "Well, not anymore. He belongs to Jesus."

We had never said anything to the energumen about the speculation that Peter might have been possessed. Years later, it was just a spontaneous boast from the demons. Was Peter possessed when Jesus chose him? Who knows? Jesus sees beyond the appearances; He saw something beautiful in Mary of Magdala and Peter the fisherman, and He called them.

Exorcist Diary 29

Divine Grace or Demonic Trick?

We were doing an exorcism that was pretty challenging. At one point, as the team was picking the woman up to bring her to the session, a luminous, almond-shaped image with a cross on top appeared on her garage. It was clearly not natural. There was no light source, no shadows, nothing to explain its appearance. It happened a second time, later in the process, as well.

Was it a grace from God to encourage us? Or was it a ploy from Satan? In the midst of an exorcism, our rule is to assume any supernatural occurrence is demonic unless proven otherwise, especially if the possessed individual has an active spiritual life. We assume Satan is trying to manipulate the person, as is usually the case. Moreover, Satan is amazingly adept at mimicking supernatural realities (appearing as an "angel of light" [2 Cor. 11:14]) so one often cannot tell immediately whether it is God's grace or Satan's ploy.

We never did determine the source of this image. It was seemingly not of this world. If it was Satan's ploy, he wasted a lot of energy because it had no real impact. We generally took it as an encouragement from God, which is always welcome. Eventually, the possessed woman was liberated. But I kept a photo of the image.

Exorcist Diary 30

Demons Texting Us

Demons love tech, just like adolescents. Before the cell phone was invented, demons would mess with lights or the television or other electrical appliances in a house (and still do). People would come to us saying their house was infested because the electronics would turn off and on and do wild things by themselves. Sometimes they had faulty wiring, but other times it was indeed demonic.

Now our team members, especially the priest exorcists, are getting *text messages* from demons. I have heard that other exorcists around the world are also starting to get them.[22] The messages are typically snarky, arrogant, gloating, and taunting. Of course, we don't engage in a conversation with demons.

Recently a prominent priest denied the existence of a personal evil. He accepted a kind of abstract notion of evil but not evil beings with real personhood, meaning Satan and other demons. All I can say is, *he never got a text from a demon!* That might change his mind.

[22] Cathy Cañares Yamsuan, "'Demonic Texts': The Enemy Can Use Technology, Says Exorcist," *Inquirer.net*, November 1, 2020, https://newsinfo.inquirer.net/1354888/demonic-texts-the-enemy-can-use-technology-says-exorcist.

Demons are enamored by tech. They engage in their demonic antics to scare us and to make themselves seem powerful. In reality, they are just the antics of an immature adolescent. Demons have no wisdom; they rejected God. They have much more raw intelligence than we do, but, without wisdom, they are shallow.

Demonic texts only confirm for us the presence of demons. Their biggest asset is their invisibility, and it is stupid for them to blow this cover by calling attention to themselves. At times, they can't help it. They are very impulsive and cannot control their vicious, gloating sadism.

I was glad we received these texts; it is self-defeating behavior. It lets us know where they are acting. When they expose themselves, I counsel the priests to respond with a prayer. All I can say to these demons is: Send more!

Theological Reflection

Demons Can Text?

The demonic assaults against saints and mystics are well known and documented. For example, the infernal attacks against Padre Pio were so intense that the other friars in his community thought he might be possessed and considered an exorcism. St. Gemma Galgani (1878–1903) likewise suffered such intense demonic attacks that she repeatedly asked for an exorcism, although it was not necessary for her either. It can be difficult to discern the difference between demonic attacks on a victim soul and those of a possessed person.

Also noteworthy are the subtle manipulations and deceits of Satan against holy souls. For example, Satan disguised himself as Padre Pio's spiritual director in an attempt to deceive him. Similarly, Satan disguised himself as the local bishop and appeared to St. Veronica Giuliani (1660–1727), a mystic Capuchin nun, and told her that her entire life was a complete diabolical illusion.[23]

Demons can also manipulate material objects. For example, it is not uncommon in infested houses for sacred objects to fly off the walls, for holy objects to break, and for windows and shutters to slam shut. It is also not uncommon for electronics to act up; for instance,

---

[23] Filippo Maria Salvatori, *The Life of St. Veronica Giuliani, Capuchin Nun* (London: R. Washbourne, 1874), 184.

televisions and lights might turn on and off seemingly by themselves.

Demons will mess with anything they can in their attempt to frighten, intimidate, and show off their "power." In this modern digital age, they manipulate computers and cell phones. It is not unusual for possessed people to find it difficult to speak to their exorcist on their cell phones because of demonic interference. Their computers might crash for no reason. And, as the above diary entry attests, demons will even send threatening messages via text. I have personally received a number of these, and I know of several others who have as well.

If demons formerly manipulated televisions and lights, why would they not do the same now with computers and cell phones? The answer is: they do!

Exorcist Diary 31

Sanctus, Sanctus, Sanctus

I had an intense session today. The individual said that, during the week, the words "I am God" spontaneously came out of her mouth. Being a good Christian, this was distressing for her. We recommended she do her best to ignore this obvious demonic rant. We have heard the same demonic boast coming out of the mouths of the possessed more than a few times.

During the session, when it came time for the "Sanctus, sanctus, sanctus" (Holy, holy, holy) in the Rite, the demons reacted strongly. These words come straight from the Bible and describe the praise of God by the angels (Isa. 6:3; Rev. 4:8). This was the song the demons refused to sing. The fallen angels refused to praise God and thus denied their own true nature.

While all demons typically find the chanting of the "Sanctus, sanctus, sanctus" odious, the group of demons we were addressing was especially strongly affected. These demons were stuck on the idea that they are "God," and they reject praising the one true God.

So, we stuck with that phrase for much of the session: "Holy, holy, holy." It worked, and they reacted wildly. I reminded them that this was the song they refused to sing, and yet it was their song. I also used the battle cry of St. Michael in casting out

Lucifer and his demons: *Quis ut Deus?* — "Who is like God?" And, of course, the answer is, no one.

Praising God is the joy of the angels, and it is our joy as well: "Holy, holy, holy is the Lord God of hosts!"

Theological Reflection

The 1614 Rite of Exorcism versus the Post–Vatican II Rite

When a priest is given the express faculties to conduct a solemn exorcism by his bishop, the core instrument that he uses is the Church's Rite of Exorcism. He will employ other holy instruments when they seem to be effective, such as holy water and relics of saints, but the focus of the exorcism session will be on the Rite of Exorcism.

The exorcist may use the pre–Vatican II Rite of Exorcism, which was published in 1614. It is prayed in Latin. It is thought that Latin, being the ancient language of the Church, has a special efficacy in casting out demons.

The 1614 Rite was a codification of the experiences of exorcists down through the centuries. It codified what worked, based upon their experience. An exorcist is not concerned much with liturgical niceties. Rather, he wants a ritual that works, and the 1614 is very effective.

Exorcists may also use the revised Rite of Exorcism that was promulgated after the Second Vatican Council. The initial revision, available in 1999, was the focus of much criticism. Many exorcists around the world complained that it took much of the "teeth" out of the Rite, especially with fewer imperative prayers that command the demons to leave.

In addition to other prayers, the 1614 Rite of Exorcism has three long imprecatory prayers with multiple commands for the demons to depart. The revised Rite has only one imprecatory prayer, and the revised Rite is focused more on mirroring the sacrament of Baptism.

I would characterize the difference this way: the 1614 Rite is an unabashed and continued pummeling of the demons' presence. The revised Rite seems to be, at least partly, renewing the sacrament of Baptism and its cleansing power in the afflicted person.

I have used the revised Rite, and it does work in casting out demons. The Church's Rite and the priest are given the requisite spiritual authority, and so it is naturally efficacious. Also, there are additional imprecatory prayers in the appendix, commanding the demons to leave, which I often include when using the revised Rite. So the exorcist can augment the revised Rite with additional prayers with "teeth." Nevertheless, the 1614 Rite of Exorcism in Latin remains the general favorite of exorcists.

Exorcist Diary 32

"The Look"

One of the common signs we use to diagnose a demonic presence is "the look." When the person comes in, he or she typically appears normal. But when we start to pray, if there is an evil spirit, it will likely manifest within the first twenty minutes. Before beginning to thrash in reaction to the prayers, there may appear on the person's face "the look."

This look is something impossible to fake or for a human being to imitate. The look is one of overwhelming rage and pure evil. It can be unnerving staring into a demon's eyes and seeing such evil and a desire to destroy. Wow! When you see it, there is no question in your mind: this person is possessed!

The eyes tell it all. If God allowed the demons complete freedom, which He doesn't, the demons would torture you mercilessly and rip you apart. I am aware of mystics who have had visions of Hell, a place where demons are unchained. The mystics describe their awful tortures. It is all pretty upsetting, as it should be. There are some difficult parts of this ministry, and staring into the eyes of raging evil is one of them.

·

Exorcist Diary 33

Casting Out Demons of Fear

This week, one of our graced team members was praying in the middle of the night, a time when the work of the Spirit is particularly clear. She was overwhelmed with a feeling of fear. It was a powerful experience.

She knew what she was called to do. She offered the fear to God, again and again. She gave the fear to the Immaculate and Sacred Hearts, there to be burned up and made harmless. Again and again throughout the hour, she offered this overwhelming fear and panic to their hearts. And again and again, it was burned up by holy fire. Through the night's holy hour, she prayed, "Jesus, I trust in You. Jesus, I trust in You." Finally, at the end of the hour, it was over. Peace returned.

It seems clear that there was, in that hour, a grace for all of us. Fear is gripping our nation and the world. Evil spirits of fear, panic, and terror are everywhere, trying to destroy our trust in God. The solution is clear: commend it all to the Sacred and Immaculate Hearts. In those holy hearts, fear will be destroyed. During it all, we should often say, "Jesus, I trust in You."

In the end, peace will be restored. Of that, there is no doubt.

Exorcist Diary 34

Demons in Exorcisms Recite Our Sins?

Often when people are invited to join exorcism teams, including priests, they are concerned that the demons will tell their sins in the middle of the session. Does it happen, or is this just Hollywood hype?

It does happen. The demons like to focus especially on the exorcist's sins and thus discourage his efforts. We have even had sessions in which the demons bring up past sins, previously confessed. (Some say the demons cannot recite sins that have been confessed, but that hasn't been our experience.) It seems that God has limited demons in what sins they can recite, so we don't get it daily, and their recital is limited.

How to respond? Normally, we ignore whatever comes from a demon's mouth. But the sins they mention are often right on target, so it is not good to deny it. Denial and lying are something demons do, not Christians.

Rather, my response is always the same: "It is true. I am a sinner. But I am not your problem. Jesus is your problem. And it is in His holy name that I cast you out." When we honestly confess our sins, Satan's power is broken.

Some saints have experienced these demonic encounters at the end of their lives as they lay dying. Satan came and recited their sins and demanded that they belong to him. But the saints looked to Jesus and asked forgiveness. They knew it was His mercy, and only His mercy, that saved them.

At the hour of our death, and even now, we ought to do the same.

Exorcist Diary 35

Heavy Demons

Gemma Galgani, mystic, stigmatist, and saint, wasted away and died presumably from tuberculosis. She certainly weighed less than a hundred pounds at the end of her life. Yet, four days before she died, several strong workmen could not move her. Gemma's response was, "It is not I, you know, that weigh so."[24] She was mercilessly assaulted by demons, and their oppressive presence held her down. Once she died, she was easily lifted.

We have had possessed individuals who, in the midst of their manifesting a demonic presence, were unexplainably heavy and well-nigh impossible to move. One of the classic signs of possession includes preternatural strength. This is usually interpreted to mean that the person exhibits a strength beyond his or her natural abilities, which often makes the person hard to restrain in an exorcism.

This sign of superhuman strength is much broader, though. It refers to physical effects in the individual that cannot be humanly accounted for but can be explained by a demonic presence. For example, levitation is just such a sign. A human being cannot

---

[24] *The Saint Gemma Galgani Collection*, chap. 30 (London: Catholic Way Publishing, 2013), Kindle ed., 510.

naturally levitate, but demons can use their natural abilities to lift someone off the ground, and occasionally they do.

We are careful in diagnosing possession. But sometimes there is no other reasonable explanation. I read fairly often that some people do not believe in angels or demons, Satan or Hell. Sometimes even priests do not believe such things. I often think that a day or two with Gemma Galgani or in the chapel of an exorcist would likely change their minds.

Theological Reflection

Demons Affecting the Material World

Demons are purely spiritual beings, as are angels. Normally, angelic and demonic influence on human beings is through suggestion and attempting to influence a person's mind and body. Our guardian angel inspires us to do good; demons tempt us to do evil. But both the angels and the demons have no control over our human will and freedom. In the end, we alone are responsible for the choices we make.

Angels and demons can and do occasionally manipulate objects within the material world to help or harm us.[25] For example, demons are known for throwing objects off the wall of an infested house, or other such physical antics. Of course, they are allowed to do only what God permits. Otherwise, Satan would wreak even more havoc than he already does.

The great mystics, such as Padre Pio and St. Gemma Galgani, were physically assaulted by demons. They were also helped by angels. I found it particularly humorous and inspiring when St. Gemma claimed in her diary that after a particularly horrendous night of demonic attacks, her guardian angel got her a cup of coffee in the morning. (I am waiting for my angel to do this!)[26]

---

[25] See St. Thomas Aquinas, *ST*, I, q. 110.
[26] "My guardian angel does not cease to watch over me.... Many times during the day he reveals himself

Thus, we see that demons can, and do, enter and manipulate the material world to a limited extent. This includes interfering with our phones and communication devices. They attempt to isolate, harass, and frighten. The best response is simply remain calm and respond with a prayer.

I am convinced that such material interventions "cost" the demons dearly, as their spiritual power and energy are not infinite. Thus, they interfere only with targets they have a special interest in. So, if the demons are directly intervening in your communications, give thanks that you have been found "worthy" of such harassment and offer any related sacrifice to God.

---

to me and talks to me. Yesterday he kept me company while I ate but he didn't force me like the others do. After I had eaten, I didn't feel at all well so he brought me a cup of coffee so good that I was healed instantly and then he made me rest a little." *Diary of Saint Gemma Galgani*, pt. 4, Monday, August 20, 1900, in *The Saint Gemma Galgani Collection*, 4 vols. (Catholic Way Publishing, 2013), p. 134, Kindle ed.

Exorcist Diary 36

Stuck in Unforgiveness

During the process of an exorcism, sometimes people get stuck. We pray and pray and pray, and they don't seem to get any better. Why are they not being liberated?

What sometimes emerges is a deep-seated lack of forgiveness. Many of those who come to us with demonic spirits have been traumatized in their youth by someone. They are understandably angry and harbor an inner desire for their tormentor to suffer. But as long as they hang on to that anger and unforgiveness, it is they who are being poisoned.

Demons latch onto this and will not leave. The demons themselves are forever stuck in an inner rage. They are spending an eternity in Hell blaming God (unjustly) and holding on to their anger and resentment.

One of the problems in our culture is that people misunderstand what it means to forgive. It does *not* mean we condone others' evil behavior. It does *not* mean that abusers should not answer for their crimes and go to prison. It does *not* mean we should have a warm feeling and have a positive emotional connection to our abusers.

Rather, forgiveness in the Christian sense is letting go of the resentment and the anger and then asking God to bless the person who has offended us. It is a decision. Jesus loved and forgave the scribes and the Pharisees, but He called them "whitewashed tombs" and was angry at them (Matt. 23:27). Forgiveness is not an emotion; it is an act of the will.

Jesus tells us to bless and never to curse. When we curse others, it is first we ourselves who suffer. On the other hand, when we bless our enemies and those who persecute us, it is we who are liberated and at peace.

Thus, as a regular part of our exorcism process, we ask the person if there are people that he or she needs to forgive. We then have the person say something to the effect, "I willingly forgive N., and I ask God to bless N." Oftentimes the person will cry good tears. Then we know that God is healing the person's soul, and the demons will take flight.

How Do Demons Depart?

If one has the mystic charism of seeing demons, then one can see them leave. There are a very few people with such a gift. The rest of us must surmise based on a number of typical signs.

As demons get weaker, they begin to cry and whine. In the beginning, they are arrogant and haughty. Initially, they look at the exorcist with a sneer and tell him that he has no authority and no power. They emphatically state that they will never leave. A seasoned exorcist will recognize this as empty bluster and know that the demons are actually terrified.

As they get weaker, demons will sometimes reveal their names, such as Legion, Beelzebul, Baal, or a myriad of other demonic names. Having the name in hand gives the exorcist additional power, and he knows that the demons are on the ropes.

Demons are typically present in a kind of hierarchical colony. There are often many present in a true case of possession. They usually run in packs. Each section has its own leader with one leader in charge of them all.

As the entire colony becomes weaker and starts to leave, the weakest, smallest ones leave first. Then the exorcist gets to the leader of a particular cohort. When that leader goes, the rest of his cohort go with him.

Eventually, the leader of them all will depart. He will be the most powerful of the demons in the entire colony. He may leave with a bang, a flash of light, or some other loud manifestation, or maybe not. The afflicted person will often convulse wildly and repeatedly. The person may vomit a great deal of white foam.

The exorcist will be cautious, since the demons often fake leaving and try to remain hidden. This is a common tactic.

When the demons finally leave, the afflicted persons will come to and be fully conscious. They will be exhausted but feel a great sense of relief. They will say they feel lighter, perhaps even freed. They typically know that some demons left, although they are not likely to know for certain if they all left.

Once the highest-ranking demon has been exorcised, it is over. At this point, exorcists will want to stay in touch with the individuals to ensure that the demons are truly gone.

Moreover, the exorcists will want the individuals to continue under the pastoral care of their local pastors or similar individuals to ensure they continue on the road of holy living and do not offer an opening for the demons to return.

Exorcist Diary 37

The New Light Bearer

Lucifer, the Light Bearer or Morning Star (Isa. 14:12), lost his elevated position in the angelic hierarchy. Some theologians speculate that he was first among the angels. He was certainly the leader of the angelic rebellion that Michael and his angels cast out of Heaven.

Mary is the new Light Bearer. Jesus is the Light. Only she who is immaculate and perfectly humble could contain such divine holiness. Anything stained would find such infinite light unbearable.

Thus, it is she, the new Light Bearer, who now casts out Lucifer. In one case we had in which Lucifer himself was personally present, Mary appeared at the end and cast him out. Whenever she appears, bearing the light of Christ, demons flee.

There is no true exorcist or exorcism team that does not rely heavily on Mary. She figures prominently in the Rite of Exorcism, new and old. She is our Light Bearer; she is our Morning Star.

Theological Reflection

The Role of Mary, the Mother of Jesus

It is expected that a Catholic exorcist would have a strong devotion to the Blessed Virgin Mary, the Mother of Jesus. After Jesus Himself, she is the strongest ally of the exorcist.

Mary is commonly thought to be the woman in the book of Revelation who is "clothed with the sun, with the moon under her feet, and on her head a crown of twelve stars" (12:1). Genesis 3:15 is typically applied to her as well: "I will put enmity between you and the woman"—in which she, through the power of her Son, crushes the head of the serpent, who is Satan. Thus, the Church's current Rite of Exorcism invokes Mary while commanding the demons to flee: "The exalted Virgin Mary, Mother of God, commands you, she who in her lowliness crushed your proud head" (69). I recently used this line during an exorcism, and the demons reacted very strongly. Clearly, the statement had a powerful effect.

The popular Marian tradition of the Catholic Church believes that Mary has an ongoing, definitive role in casting out Satan. Many exorcists report that whenever the Virgin Mary appears in the midst of an exorcism, the demons are immediately overcome. She is "full of grace," and the grace of Christ in her has completely conquered Satan. Thus, Satan and his demons are no match for her.

The demons hate her so much that they will refuse to speak her name but refer to her only as "that woman" or some such abstraction. Her name, like Jesus', is considered holy and is itself odious to the demons and a grace for those who utter it with devotion.

Exorcist Diary 38

Two Become One

Some time ago, we had a woman who was manifesting demonic symptoms. Upon deeper investigation, it became clear that the "open door" to the demonic came through her husband. The husband had the moral problem, not the wife. Yet the wife was manifesting demonic symptoms.

Thus, it was important to have the married couple present when we performed the deliverance prayers. The wife would have a hard time being freed without her husband's cooperation and conversion. As a matter of course, we like to have both husband and wife present for any prayer sessions.

The sacrament of Marriage speaks of the two spouses becoming one. Our experience suggests this is a reality. Spouses become one flesh and share intimately their ups and downs, graces and failures. They should pray together, worship together, and support each other on the path to holiness. And before one spouse engages in any untoward behavior, he or she might consider the harm it can cause to both spouses.

Exorcist Diary 39

Don't Dialogue with the Devil

Pope Francis has repeatedly warned people against talking to Satan. He said, "If you start talking to Satan you are lost.... He is more intelligent than us."[27] Indeed, Satan is the father of lies and a master manipulator of the human psyche. Thus, the pope admonishes us not to address Satan directly, except to tell him to leave.

Perhaps the only exception is during an exorcism. In such cases, the exorcist may command the demons to say their names, tell how they entered an individual, answer when they will leave, and reveal any other information directly related to the mission of casting the demons out. But he should ask no more.

One day I made a mistake. The demon said he was Lucifer. Later, the name Satan surfaced. I asked him, "Are they the same entity?" The response was, "They are the same." I then recalled something I had just read; Fr. Gabriele Amorth, the famous exorcist of Rome, had said he thought they were different entities. So I said as much: "Fr. Amorth said they are two different beings."

27 Max Rossi, "Satan Is 'More Intelligent Than Us,' Don't Converse with Him—Pope Francis," RT, December 13, 2017, https://www .rt.com/news/413020-pope-francis-devil-satan/.

A mistake. I had veered into an area of curiosity which, in this case, is a low-level sin of pride. This gave the demons an opening, and they jumped at it. For the next twenty-four hours, I was pummeled with demonic obsessions in my head—all sorts of wild temptations and attacks. Fortunately, with repentance and prayer, these attacks finally stopped.

Pope Francis's admonition against talking to Satan is important, not only because Satan will outwit us, but also it will give him an opening into our heads. Being pummeled by demonic obsessions is no fun, at best. At worst, it can lead to dire consequences. I assure you, I am now much more careful not to cross the line.

Interrogating Demons

When demons fully manifest in a possessed person, they may take over the personality of the individual for a limited time. When this happens, the afflicted individual's personality recedes into the background. Some demons are mute, and so they do not speak. But many do.

What comes out of the mouth of the possessed person when controlled by demons are typically ugly, negative, and accusatory lies. I often instruct new exorcists, and the possessed especially, to remember that everything out of a demon's mouth is a lie or a manipulation.

With his authority over demons, however, the exorcist can command the demons to tell the truth. If they are weak enough or if God wills it, then they are forced to tell the truth. It is then that the exorcist can gather valuable information to assist in the exorcism.

As noted previously, the exorcist will appropriately ask how many demons are present and the names of the leaders, how they entered the person, what it will take to cast them out, when they are leaving, and other information directly relevant to the exorcism.

It is not appropriate for the exorcist to ask for information unrelated to the exorcism, especially to satisfy his theological curiosity. This gives the demons an opening into the exorcist himself, and he will likely find the exorcism going awry and the demons attacking his brain through demonic obsession.

Exorcist Diary 40

No Deals with Demons

In the midst of an exorcism, the "out front" demon said, "I will make a deal with you."

I responded, "You want to make a deal? I'll make a deal with you. Here's the deal: you leave."

No response.

An hour or so later, that demon left with his underlings. He knew he was on the ropes and was trying to cut a deal.

There is only one group worse to make a deal with than terrorists, and that's demons. They manipulate, and they lie. Even if Satan promises you something, he may not deliver and will claim your soul in the process.

Over the years, we have exorcised a number of people who have made deals with Satan in one form or another. Some have made explicit pacts in Satanic rituals. Others have done so unwittingly through occult practices. Asking a witch or shaman to grant you a favor, such as healing or wealth or having another fall in love with you, is tantamount to making a deal with Satan. Such a deal will never end well.

There is a cure, however. The Cross of Jesus Christ can cancel out any pact with Satan, regardless of what Satan or anyone says. The person must be truly repentant and ask God for forgiveness and help. Once the sin is confessed and absolved, the pact is annuled and the person is returned to God's grace.

This does not mean, however, that any oppressing or possessing demons will leave easily. It may involve a rather long battle. The person is already saved, but casting out any attaching demons will typically not be quick.

The takeaway is simple: making deals with demons is a really, really bad idea.

Exorcist Diary 41

No Good Witches

A young man in his thirties came in for help. He said he had been practicing witchcraft for seven years and had started his own coven. He added, "There are a lot of covens in this area." He held on to his practice of witchcraft because he said it gave him power. But he was afraid he was becoming possessed.

There was indeed a darkness around him. He was sullen and withdrawn. I pointed out that his occult practices were slowly dragging him into the darkness. He agreed and said he knew this was true.

He came for a few sessions and then stopped; he didn't want to give up witchcraft. We pray for him.

It has become popular in some modern circles to practice witchcraft and to use spells and curses. There are many websites, movies, and other media on this topic, even for children. Disney has a children's cartoon with a teenager who battles evil through the power of her witchcraft.

A witch's or warlock's power comes from Satan. Though some practitioners might claim to be channeling some sort of good "energy" and think of themselves as "good witches," any power they have comes from the evil one, regardless of their intention. The power to cast spells and curses does not come from God.

As Deuteronomy says, "Let there not be found among you anyone who ... practices divination, or is a soothsayer, augur, or sorcerer, or who casts spells, consults ghosts and spirits, or seeks oracles from the dead. Anyone who does such things is an abomination to the LORD" (Deut. 18:10–12).

Jesus said, "Love your enemies." He said, "Bless those who curse you" (Luke 6:27–28). True Christians never curse anyone, nor do they try to obtain any good except from the hands of God.

Witchcraft is a violation of the first commandment and is very spiritually dangerous. The fact that it is being widely promoted even among children is frightening. There are many reasons for the current spike in requests for exorcisms today. This is one of them.

Exorcist Diary 42

Branded by Satan

Jason woke up with a very ugly four-inch upside-down cross burned deeply into his shoulder. Strangely, he said he didn't feel it; he just felt a little tingling. Four days later it rapidly disappeared.

Jason had foolishly asked Satan for success in his business and finances, in addition to his many other sinful behaviors. Years later, he repented and returned to the Church. But Satan had not forgotten him and was now laying claim to him. At night, Jason hears the voice of Satan in his head, "You belong to me."

The upside-down cross is a mockery of the Cross of Christ. The fact of its appearance without pain and impossible rapid healing attest to its preternatural origin. As with the branding of an animal, Satan was claiming ownership.

In the midst of the exorcism sessions using the new Rite of Exorcism, Jason repeated his baptismal vows. He rejected Satan and all his works. I had Jason explicitly add three times, "I belong to Jesus. Jesus is my Lord and Savior."

In the Rite of Baptism for infants, the priest prays, "I claim you for Christ our Savior by the sign of the cross." Echoing these sacramental words, I then prayed over Jason, "I invoke the power of the keys of Peter and by the authority of the Church, I break any covenants between Jason and the evil one. The death and

Resurrection of Jesus cancel any ownership Satan may believe he had over him. I claim Jason for Christ our Savior. In the holy name of Jesus, I set him free."

At root, an exorcism is a rejection of Satan's claim of ownership. In Baptism, we are claimed for Christ our Savior. The new Rite of Exorcism is a renewal of the sacrament of Baptism and once more frees a soul from Satan's grasp. I have come away from these experiences with a more profound appreciation and gratitude for the sacrament of Baptism and its power to free us from the evil one.

Exorcist Diary 43

Are Terrorists Possessed?

There has sprung up in these days the "lone-wolf terrorist" who commits heinous acts of violence against the innocent, including children, and then kills himself. Who would do such senseless, evil things? Some surmise that these terrorists must be possessed. Others suggest that these shooters are mentally ill. But recent studies suggest many of them do *not* have a diagnosable mental illness. Nor are they psychotic.

One study found that the majority of these perpetrators had experienced "early childhood traumas and exposure to violence."[28] This has led some of them to suffer from anxiety, depression, or suicidal thinking, or some combination of these. I have treated hundreds of people who suffer from such things, however, and none of them went on to murder innocent school children. Why did the lone-wolf terrorists end up committing such evil acts?

The study also said the shooters had become "angry and despondent" because of some perceived "grievance." Other studies

---

[28] Jillian Peterson and James Densley, "Op-Ed: We Have Studied Every Mass Shooting Since 1966. Here's What We've Learned about the Shooters," *Los Angeles Times*, August 4, 2019, https://www.latimes.com/opinion/story/2019-08-04/el-paso-dayton-gilroy-mass-shooters-data.

highlight their narcissism and desire for public notoriety. Shooters also tend to be lonely and isolated. They are often full of an internal anger and desire for revenge.

It should be noted that the emotional stance of Satan is very similar. He is in a rage and believes he has been victimized by God. He is narcissistic, arrogant, and violent. He is emotionally isolated and has no connections with other beings. He seeks revenge.

The 2014 Fort Hood shooter posted the following a few weeks before killing three people, wounding sixteen others, and then shooting himself: "I have just lost my inner peace, full of hatred, I think this time the devil will take me."[29] Perhaps he meant this only symbolically, but his emotional stance and actions are certainly in sync with what we know of the demonic. In fact, a common message that the possessed hear in their brains is a prompting to do violence to others and to kill themselves.

I do not think we can say that all of these lone-wolf terrorists are possessed. But many of them have devolved into a demonic mental state and then carry out evil actions that are very much in line with Satan's plan. We certainly should support early psychological interventions for potential shooters to deal with their underlying trauma, isolation, and rage. I suspect that some of them would likely benefit from deliverance prayers as well.

---

[29] Bryan Llenas, "Fort Hood Shooter Ivan Lopez's Chilling Facebook Post: 'The Devil Will Take Me ... Green Light and Finger Ready,'" Fox News, updated January 11, 2017, https://www.foxnews.com/world/fort-hood-shooter-ivan-lopezs-chilling-facebook-post-the-devil-will-take-me-green-light-and-finger-ready.

Theological Reflection

How Long Will It Take?

One of the most common questions I am asked by the afflicted as well as beginning exorcists is: How long will it take? They are asking how long it will take for an afflicted person to be liberated completely from the demons.

I recently heard from a man who told me he went through an exorcism and is now disappointed. He said that the exorcism "failed." By this he meant that he had one session with the exorcist and the demons didn't all leave. Many people expect the priest to wave his hands, say magic words, and all the demons will automatically depart.

In reality, an exorcism is an ugly battle. The demons have no intention of leaving a possessed person and fight to the bitter end. They are also incredibly tough and are accustomed to suffering. Despite the intense suffering they experience in an exorcism, they do not easily give up. They are like beasts with their claws in the afflicted person's body. It takes a lot of prying and effort to get them to unhook and leave.

I am consoled by the words of Fr. Gabriele Amorth: "I am content if, in a mildly serious case [of possession], a person is liberated within four or five years of exorcisms," he said. "I have had rare cases of liberations in a few months."[30]

For those who are not fully possessed but rather suffer from a lesser degree of a demonic presence, such as an oppression or an obsession, we have often found significant improvement in three to eight sessions, depending on many factors. Even these lesser cases, however, can last many months or even years before full liberation.

A case of full possession usually lasts much longer. Some people are never fully liberated in their lifetime. Others take years. Some are fortunate to be liberated in a few months. Most improve rather significantly after some intensive exorcism sessions over a few months.

It is unrealistic to think that someone who has practiced witchcraft, divination, or other occult practices over several years would be liberated quickly. Similarly, those who willingly engaged in egregious sins over many years would not likely be liberated easily. They have immersed themselves in evil for many years. It is reasonable to expect the cure to take some years as well.

The issue is really the conversion of the afflicted person who is the demonic host. Once the host is truly an inhospitable place for the demons, the demons are very likely to leave. This requires intense purification

---

[30] Larry Getlen, "How an Exorcist Priest Came Face-to-Face with the Devil Himself," *New York Post*, March 7, 2020, https://nypost.com/2020/03/07/how-an-exorcist-priest-came-face-to-face-with-the-devil-himself/.

and conversion of heart. The afflicted people need not become great saints to be liberated, but the deep ruts in their souls caused by evil practices must slowly be filled in with grace.

Not surprisingly, I have found that those who are afflicted by demons through no fault of their own tend to be liberated more quickly. But those who were explicitly dedicated to Satan, were marked for demons through occult rituals, or were liberated once and then relapsed will usually have a rough time being liberated, although it is not impossible.

Exorcist Diary 44

"We Won! He Didn't Rise!"

In the midst of a solemn exorcism, we were invoking the power of the Resurrection of Jesus, and out of the demon's mouth came a jubilant "We won! We won! He didn't rise." At this, the priests in the room spontaneously broke out into laughter. I added, "This demon needs a history lesson."

Despite everything, demons have a hard time admitting the truth. They are especially in denial about the fact that they have lost the battle and are doomed to the darkness forever.

Demons will admit the truth only under duress. To acknowledge the truth is to acknowledge Jesus, who is the Truth. This is why the Rite of Exorcism is so powerful. As one senior exorcist put it: "It's like pouring the Truth down their throats." It constantly reminds them of their defeat.

Demons are blind to the world of grace. They cannot "see" grace or understand its working. Most importantly, they do not "see" the Resurrection. The resurrected Christ is perceived by the eyes of faith. Demons are spiritually blind (Acts 10:41).

We know by the eyes of our faith that Christ is risen, and this is a real seeing. Because of this, there resides in our hearts a great hope that ultimately bursts into joy. Among demons, there is neither.

Exorcist Diary 45

Exorcists Attacked by Clients' Demons

One of the priests involved in the famous exorcism of Anneliese Michel in Germany reported smelling a "variety of stenches" and became nauseated just reading a letter from the possessed woman. At night, he felt "sorely oppressed" until he invoked the intercession of Padre Pio and the weight lifted.

It is not uncommon for exorcists, particularly those with spiritual sensitivities, to experience demonic symptoms when working with possessed people. The demons are enraged that an exorcist has come to cast them out, and they attempt to attack viciously, within the parameters of what God allows. Typically, the exorcist is protected from serious harm, but he may experience some harassment.

The experience of harassment and its symptoms can actually be very helpful. It helps the exorcist know that the person really does have a demonic problem and that the problems are not just psychological. Also, the symptoms the exorcist experiences in the harassment may give him some information about the type of demons involved and what to target during subsequent sessions. Finally, the modest suffering of the priest as a result will likely, in God's providence, be of some spiritual aid for the final liberation of the afflicted soul. Thus, it is part of his ministry.

Exorcists are protected. Moreover, God does not allow Satan to kill people, including exorcists. Otherwise, Satan would kill every one of us. But exorcists can experience some demonic harassment related to specific cases. This is a grace, albeit at times, a difficult one.

Can Demons Physically Harm Us?

People who first start thinking about exorcisms and the reality of Satan are often frightened. They are afraid of what Satan will do to them. This is true even of some priests! More than a few priests have been asked by their bishops to do an exorcism, and they declined, being afraid of getting into Satan's sights.

This is nonsense. Fallen angels, or demons, can do only what God allows them to do. God allows them to tempt everyone, to possess and oppress some, and to harass a few based on God's holy designs. Even the demons ultimately do God's will and redound to God's glory, much to their chagrin.

Thus, there are limits to what demons can do. They are not allowed directly to kill us or normally to maim us permanently. In fact, during exorcism sessions, there seems to be a kind of bubble around the exorcist, and the possessed person sometimes lunges at them but stops short. The possessed person might reach out to choke the priest but will be unable to do so, as if there is an invisible shield around him. God sets boundaries.

But demons can do all sorts of tempting and even more explicit attacks. St. Thomas wrote about the malice, envy, and hatred that induces demons to tempt humans and to assault them.[31] The Church's history is

---

[31] *ST*, I, q. 114, arts. 1, 2.

full of countless examples of great saints and mystics who have suffered direct attacks by Satan and his demons.

Padre Pio, St. John Vianney, St. Gemma Galgani, St. Catherine of Siena, and many, many others suffered bruises, bloody noses, cuts, scratches, punches, kicks, and direct demonic thrashings. They endured these extraordinary trials in faith and thus achieved high degrees of sanctity. Moreover, as specially chosen victim souls, they became a conduit for the salvation of many, imitating and bonded to the Cross of Jesus.

The key is that demons can do only what God allows them to do. It is for the Christian to trust in God. Most people will not be asked to endure the extraordinary assaults of Satan. Demons will not physically beat up the vast majority of Christians. But all of us must endure his daily temptations. Like the saints, when we endure these trials with faith, God's grace triumphs in us. In the process, we become holy and are transformed into God's "little saints."

Exorcist Diary 46

Why Should You Be Anxious?

In today's session, I got spit at—again. It reminds me of something every exorcist learns very quickly: demons hate priests! Actually, it is not me they hate. They hate Jesus. When they see a priest, they see Jesus and lash out with their entire being in a raging fury. Ironically, their hatred and violence serve only to do God's will.

Satan enticed people to kill Jesus, and it was Satan's own undoing. I try to offer the spitting, the cussing, and the other insults I receive from their mouths for the liberation of the souls we pray over. The evil and violence of demons, by its very nature, is self-defeating.

As the years pass, I feel a greater sense of calm through it all. No matter what happens, Jesus wins. No matter what the demons do, they lose. It is inevitable.

It's like watching a baseball game and knowing ahead of time that your team will win—big! In that case, you can sit back and enjoy the game.

This should be the lot of all those who follow Jesus. Relax. Jesus wins, and we win with Him. Why should you be anxious at all?

.

Exorcist Diary 47

Demons of Depression

As a licensed psychologist, I have treated many people who are clinically depressed. There are many kinds of depressions, and most are treatable. Typically, a combination of medications and psychotherapy is effective. But there are a few depressive disorders that are treatment resistant, for a variety of reasons.

A while ago, the team and I were praying over a person who had extensive involvement in the occult. At one point, one of our spiritually gifted people in the room said, "You seem to have a spirit of depression hanging on to you." The afflicted person confirmed that he was recently suffering acutely from depression. I had him say: "I renounce any evil spirits of depression, and, in Jesus' name, I command them to leave." (Laity have authority over their own bodies and can command demons to leave them in Jesus' name).

I then affirmed it: "As a representative of the Church, I invoke the keys of St. Peter, and I command the demons of depression to leave." Within seconds, he felt the depression lift, and he was much better and has remained so.

An increasing exposure to the demonic brings with it a darkness, heaviness, and a depressive effect. Though it looks like a depression, it typically does not respond to medications or psychotherapy. As we continue to invoke the healing power of Jesus and command evil spirits to leave, one solid sign of improvement is the lifting of a darkness around the person and an increasing sense of light, joy, and peace.

When someone is depressed, our first intervention is to suggest seeing a mental health professional and perhaps a psychiatrist to prescribe medication. But if that doesn't work and there are signs of a demonic presence, then strong deliverance prayers, including a command to the demons of depression to leave, might be in order.

Exorcist Diary 48

Sickening Crystals

One of my spiritual directees said that she has not been feeling well. A well-intentioned Christian friend had given her some crystals. She was told the crystals would help her health. Since then, she has been feeling particularly ill.

She told me about the crystals, and I told her to bring them to me. I then blessed and disposed of them. She instantly started to feel better. The crystals were making her sick.

So many people think of themselves as doing good but are involved in occult practices that invoke evil powers. Good witches? Healing crystals? White magic? If it doesn't directly involve God, then the only other option is Satan's power, and that is not good — regardless of one's intentions.

Theological Reflection

Occult Practices Invite Demons In

The Bible is very clear about its condemnation of occult practices: "Let there not be found among you anyone who ... practices divination, or is a soothsayer, augur, or sorcerer, or who casts spells, consults ghosts and spirits, or seeks oracles from the dead. Anyone who does such things is an abomination to the LORD" (Deut. 18:10–12).

The *Catechism* echoes this prohibition and says that any violation is a violation of the First Commandment and an offense against the worship due to God alone. "All forms of divination are to be rejected: recourse to Satan or demons, conjuring up the dead ... astrology, palm reading ... recourse to mediums ... All practices of magic or sorcery ... Wearing charms is also reprehensible" (CCC 2116–2117).

Using crystals to ward off demons, cast spells, or invoke occult healing energy clearly falls under this prohibition. This is sinful, occult behavior that creates an opening for demons. A person who engages in such behavior might argue that he or she didn't realize what was happening. The response is clear, "You should have known."

Exorcist Diary 49

Whose Voice in Your Head?

In the midst of sessions, the demons often ridicule and verbally put down people in the room, especially the exorcist. They try to tear us down, even using sacred symbols. In the past, they have criticized me for many things: "You don't say Mass everyday" (I missed a few days); "Some of you here did not go to confession today" (the demon then mentioned the names of every person in the room who hadn't); "You didn't kiss your stole before you put it on" (priests traditionally kiss the cross on the stole before putting it on).

The demons are not concerned about the quality of my spiritual life. They are trying to tear down my self-esteem. Ironically, I now make sure I kiss the cross on my stole; I go to confession every week; I say Mass every day, no matter the circumstances.

We all have little voices in our ears. Daily we hear messages; some build us up, but many try to tear us down. The latter tell us that we are not measuring up; we are not good enough; we are alone, and no one cares; there is no hope for us. These voices try to shame us. These are messages from Satan, no matter how disguised in religious symbolism they might be.

God's message to us is one of love and support. God tells us that we are loved and we are forgiven. We are welcomed into the Kingdom. God never stops looking at us and communicating messages of love and mercy.

Take a moment during the day and pay attention to the messages you are hearing inside your head. If a message builds you up in joy and peace, it comes from God. If it tears you down, it is Satan's voice. Whenever the latter comes, reject the evil one and turn in confidence to your loving Father.

America Needs Deliverance

I love America, but it needs help. We typically do assessments of individuals who may have demonic activity. If one were to assess our country as a whole right now, there are strong signs that our country is demonically oppressed.

First, there are plenty of openings for the demonic. There is a significant drop in the practice of the Faith. This causes a critical loss of graced protection. Moreover, many people are practicing witchcraft and wicca, playing with Ouija boards, and engaging in occult practices that open the door to the demonic. There are close to a million abortions each year in the United States, and we have found this to be a huge demonic door. And there are other sinful behaviors on the rise, such as Internet pornography, drug and sexual addictions, and more. Sin gives evil increasing access to our lives.

Second, there are signs in our country of a demonic mentality infecting our communities. One of the first signs of the demonic is discord. The level of discord in this country is through the roof. Rising levels of unhappiness, hopelessness, and suicides are also typical demonic signs; suicide rates have risen in the United States for several years (according to statistics from the CDC through 2018). Outbursts of rage, anger, and violence often accompany demonic activity; one sign of this in our country is a steady increase in terrorism. Finally, Satan and his minions think of themselves as victims, and a victim mentality is increasingly pervasive in the United States.

These are disturbing trends that point to an increasing influence of Satan and his minions in our country. Of course, Satan does *not* have the final word. God is in charge, and His designs will never be thwarted. Nevertheless, I believe our country is becoming increasingly demonically oppressed (not yet fully possessed!).

What to do? As with any client who is oppressed, we start with closing the doors to the demonic. Stop sinning; stop practicing the occult, and start practicing the Faith. Barring any nationwide conversion or extraordinary divine intervention, or both, this is unlikely. In fact, all trends seem to be in the wrong direction.

But all is not lost! It has always been that the small barque of Peter, with a little band of the faithful on deck, can turn back divine judgment and "coax" the Almighty into shedding extraordinary graces on the people. The redemptive graces of Jesus' death and Resurrection are infinite, and our merciful God intensely desires to shed these graces upon us.

What must we do? Love God and love the people—completely. Judge no one—left or right, liberal or conservative, Republican or Democrat, black or white. Pray constantly. Invoke the Blessed Virgin. Pray that our little prayers and sacrifices may be filled with the Spirit and share in the redemptive action of Jesus. Thus, they will become immensely fecund.

God will not abandon the United States. I believe it has a special role to play in the divine plan of salvation. But the influence of the demonic these days is palpable. The country needs us, and our prayers, right now.

Ecce Crucem Domini, Part 1

At the end of an exorcism session, I typically ask the afflicted person how it went. This provides much important information. These people give me valuable feedback on what seems to work and what most strongly affects the particular evil spirits that are present. Different demons respond differently to various sacramentals and prayers.

After a recent session, I asked the afflicted person what happened. He responded, "When you held up the crucifix, I felt something leave." He was referring to the moment the exorcist holds up the cross and commands the demons to flee. Perhaps the most famous line, and a part of the Rite of Exorcism from the earliest days, is that command: *Ecce Crucem Domini, Fugite Partes Adversae* (Behold the Cross of the Lord, take flight, you hostile powers).

I have seen Hollywood movies that parody exorcisms, and they scoff at the moment the crucifix is held up and these words of command are given. I assure you, nothing could be further from the truth. It is a powerful moment when the exorcist, as a representative of the Church founded by Jesus Himself and endowed with His full authority, holds up the sign of Satan's defeat and commands him to leave.

So many people today are ill-advisedly afraid of Satan. But if they saw the devil's terror and his abject powerlessness when forced to look upon the crucifix of Jesus, they would not be. Rather, they would reverence the infinite grace of the death and Resurrection of Jesus and would bow before the One who is truly almighty.

Exorcist Diary 52

Ecce Crucem Domini, Part 2

It is likely not an accident that what first greets pilgrims upon entering St. Peter's Square in Vatican City is the ancient exorcistic formula: *Ecce Crux Domini, Fugite Partes Adversae,* or "Behold the Cross of the Lord, take flight, you hostile powers." This powerful prayer and command is inscribed on the base of the Egyptian obelisk in the center of the square. The Holy City is the site of St. Peter's crucifixion and the residence of his successors. All who approach ought to be cleansed of evil before entering this sacred place.

This obelisk was originally built in 1835 B.C. by Pharaoh Mencares to honor the sun. The Church later placed it on this prayer pedestal and placed a large bronze cross with a relic of the true Cross on the top.[32] No doubt this pagan monument needed a spiritual cleansing!

So, too, do all of our homes. There ought to be a holy water font at the entrance to the house, for cleansing those entering the family's sanctuary. There ought to be blessed crucifixes in strategic locations, including in each bedroom. Holy pictures

---

[32] "The Obelisk," St. Peter's Basilica Info, http://stpetersbasilica. info/Exterior/Obelisk/Obelisk.htm.

of the Virgin and the family's favorite saints are very helpful. Regularly saying blessings, and even deliverance prayers, is recommended. Using these sacramentals is especially important for those who need deliverance.

There would be many fewer people coming to us for help if, from the beginning, they had availed themselves of the many protective aids the Church offers. Nevertheless, even in the direst circumstances, God forgives and generously bestows saving graces that can expel the most difficult of demons.

Exorcist Diary 53

The Young Man with the Demon Tattoo

Some time ago, a distressed father brought in his son. The son admitted a regular habit of smoking marijuana and delving into demonology. He was developing a relationship with some demons, including one he specifically named, Astaroth. He admitted to having a tattoo of Astaroth on his chest. When I asked him why he did that, he responded, "I thought it would make me a better person."

I probably do not get as upset as I should about the upside-down depictions of God, angels, and demons in the television and movie industry. Most of us older people think that it is obvious that God is good and Satan is bad. We instinctively know that the devil is evil and out to destroy us. We know God wants what is best for us, even if we do not go to Church or worship as we should.

Unfortunately, the younger generation, having had little or no basic catechesis, are easy prey for those who promote the world of Satan and his demons. Today, some espouse pagan deities and wicca; still others believe that Satan is misunderstood and is our advocate; others believe casting spells, so regularly depicted on television, is a good thing.

Unfortunately, the young man with the demon tattoo was becoming increasingly dark, resentful, and sullen. He had no intention of stopping marijuana smoking and was searching for a New Age "church" that promoted it. He didn't realize that tattooing a demon's likeness on one's body was tantamount to branding oneself to his service.

We can "decommission" tattoos through the power of Jesus. However, the young man needed a long course in theology and a conversion of his life, which he resisted. Exorcisms are not magic, and they are ineffective when the person will not desist from evil. I do not know where he is today, but, barring a powerful grace from God, I am not optimistic.

Decommissioning Tattoos

I was recently stunned to see that a young man had just acquired a tattoo of an Egyptian god—a demonic-looking figure complete with horns. As noted previously, many pagan gods are actually demons, such as Baal, who was thought to be a Canaanite god but often appears in exorcisms as a high-ranking demon (1 Cor. 10:20). Thus, this young man unknowingly branded himself to a demon of Hell.

Tattoos are common today. Unbeknownst to us, one of our energumens had an image of the Blessed Virgin Mary tattooed on her shoulder. Some believe that any tattoos are a sin. They often cite Leviticus 19:28: "Do not lacerate your bodies for the dead, and do not tattoo yourself. I am the LORD." Others believe that such Bible citations need to be taken in context and refer only to tattoos done in the context of pagan rituals and thus with pagan content.

The Catholic Church has no official position on tattoos. Tattooing an image of anything evil or related to the occult, however, is obviously a bad idea and a potential opening to the demonic. Moreover, the New Testament speaks of our bodies as temples of the Holy Spirit, and they should be treated as such (1 Cor. 6:19). Any discernment about the appropriateness of getting a tattoo should include the question: "Will this tattoo contribute in a positive way to honoring my body as a temple of the Holy Spirit?"

Should someone have a tattoo of an evil image, it should be removed if possible or, at a minimum, covered. Also, we recommend that a spiritual prayer of "decommissioning" the tattoo and any occult connection be conducted, preferably in the presence of a priest, who represents the Church. Such a ritual can be found in our app Catholic Exorcism under "Decommissioning Tattoos" (see also www.catholicexorcism.org).

Exorcist Diary 54

Demons and Suicide

When trying to discern whether someone is being directly influenced by demons, I typically ask them about thoughts going through their minds. Demons try to discourage us; they would have us give up hope; they want to destroy our self-image and tear us down. A strong demonic presence necessarily leads to such negative thoughts coursing through the afflicted person's brain.

But, most of all, Satan wants us to despair and to end our lives by suicide. This was ultimately the great sin of Judas: he despaired of God's mercy. Peter likewise sinned against Jesus by denying Him, but he returned in penitence and was saved. Whenever someone is possessed, we are especially on the watch for any suicidal tendencies.

I am not suggesting that all those who die by suicide are possessed; they are not. Nor am I suggesting that they all will suffer the same fate as Judas. These judgments we leave to God. But the goal of Satan is clear: after he torments the possessed mercilessly, he wants them to die by their own hand.

Our little exorcism team is empowered by the Church, and ultimately by Jesus, to weaken and ultimately cast out evil spirits. But our ministry is more than that. When we arrive and begin to assist desperate persons, the message communicated to them is that Jesus cares about them and loves them. He will walk with them and help them. We let them know that Jesus has triumphed over Satan and will do so for them. This brings the possessed—and all of us—hope, God's hope, which is the ultimate antidote to Satan's despair.

Paralyzed by Demons

Once again, the truth is sometimes stranger than fiction. In our ministry, we always "test the spirits" to make sure they come from God (1 John 4:1). Even the holiest people can be deceived, as some of the great mystics occasionally were.

In one of our sessions, we had an exceptionally gifted person present. Toward the end of the session, one of the demons jumped off the possessed and attacked her. (Demons can be particularly threatened by the presence of such people, and they do whatever they can to discourage them from coming back.) As the session ended, I noticed that she wasn't moving. She looked up and said, "I can't move. I can't feel my body." She was paralyzed from the neck down.

Needless to say, I was worried, although she seemed pretty calm. The other priest and I prayed over her, commanding the demon to leave. We laid hands on her head and prayed many exorcism prayers. Nothing. She couldn't move. By this time, I was really getting nervous. Is this permanent? I was starting to imagine my conversation with her husband when she arrived home in such a state.

But I refused to believe it would be permanent. God does not allow such things. Then it occurred to me that if she was paralyzed, perhaps the demon was on her spine. The team carefully rolled her limp body over. We laid hands over her spine and started to pray.

She confirmed, "Yes, the demon is on my spine." After a minute, she said, "It's gone." She stood up, completely recovered, and we all left for home. She walked out as if nothing had happened. Whew!

If someone had told me before I started in this ministry that this would happen, I wouldn't have believed it. But I was there. It did happen. Believe it!

What Can the Laity Do?

In the old days, the exorcist was a mysterious solitary figure. He showed up by himself with his black bag and performed esoteric rituals in a foreign language. Then he disappeared. Those days are over, if they ever really existed.

Today, an exorcist is usually part of a team, which includes other priests and many trained laypeople. The laypeople perform a variety of critical functions, both administratively and spiritually.

Laypeople can be the initial point of contact for someone seeking an exorcism. They can ensure that intake and permission forms are filled out and that the petitioners answer some initial questions posed by the exorcist.

Laypeople with mental-health and medical degrees can help screen the afflicted person for mental and physical illnesses and recommend appropriate kinds of health care before, during, and after the course of an exorcism. They can also advise the exorcist about mental and physical health considerations, in particular during the initial discernment, but also throughout the healing process.

We often assign a "big brother or sister" to the afflicted person to be a support during the process of an exorcism. An exorcism can be stressful and, at times, discouraging and even a source of some suffering. Having a seasoned, trained layperson as a support can help the afflicted person to understand what is happening and persevere during the process. Also, some of the laypeople, especially those with the requisite training, may be assigned as spiritual directors for the afflicted.

During the sessions themselves, laypeople are critical members of the prayer team. These "prayer warriors" pray and fast during the sessions, whether they are physically present or not. Those present will pray with the afflicted person during the exorcism session while the priest prays the solemn Rite.

As noted previously, a few of the laity will have special spiritual charisms that can assist the exorcist, especially in discernment. These spiritual sensitivities need to be carefully discerned and tested. Many long-standing exorcism teams have at least one spiritual sensitive.

Some of the physically stronger members present will provide safety for all by being available to restrain the afflicted person, if necessary. Though not all of the possessed physically manifest to the point of possible self-harm or potential harm to others, many do.

After a session, lay team members will stay with the afflicted persons, if needed, until they recover and are able to leave in a safe condition.

In our modern day, laypeople perform vital functions, spiritual and administrative, at every step of the process of an exorcism. The solitary priest exorcist has been replaced with a coordinated and trained team of laypeople, priests, and deacons.

Exorcist Diary 56

Knife in the Back

When people attend our exorcism sessions for the first time, they sometimes do not come in with a realistic understanding of the dynamics. They may have watched too many television shows depicting "nice" demons and the like.

I had a religious sister in one of the sessions, assisting for the first time. I looked at her and said, "I want you to know what you are dealing with." I then looked at the possessed person who was manifesting and said to the possessing demon: "If you could, would you knife every person here in the back, twist the knife, and laugh? In Jesus' name, I command you to tell the truth." The sullen demonic voice, forced to admit its complete perversity, reluctantly responded, "Yes."

Demons are not your friends. They even hate each other. They are vicious sadists and enjoy making people suffer. Fortunately, God does not allow them, at least on earth, to do such things. They are chained beasts (2 Thess. 2:6; Rev. 20:1–3).

But if they could, demons would knife everyone in the back and laugh.

Exorcist Diary 57

Touched by Grace … Again

Many people think of an exorcism session as an ugly encounter between the priest and the demons. The priest commands the demons to leave, and the demons resist. A battle ensues with the afflicted person screaming, writhing, and often vomiting. Actually, this is true as often as not. But it misses the big picture.

Recently, during a session, one of our faithful team members had tears of joy in her eyes. She had the courage to journey with an afflicted person not only as a "big sister" during the entire process, but also praying by her side in each session. In the midst of the session, God clearly blessed her for it and gave her a special grace.

An exorcism is a profound spiritual event. It is a powerful grace for conversion and healing, not only for the afflicted person, but for everyone in the room.

We have been given the special grace to know that at least one high-ranking angel from the rank of powers is always present. Specific saints often come to our aid. And, of course, the Queen of Heaven is very close. In an exorcism, we enter the supernatural realm of the angels and saints.

I thank God for the gift of being an exorcist and being part of Jesus' healing ministry. It is a great grace for everyone in the room. God is never outdone in generosity.

Exorcist Diary 58

Satan in Your Head

All of us suffer from demonic temptations. Lures and entice-ments are just what Satan does. At times, no matter how much we protect ourselves through prayer and proper living, it seems Satan may get into the heads of our exorcists and wreak havoc.

Last night, one of our exorcists was bombarded with intense thoughts of guilt and self-recrimination. It started subtly, but then rose to an intense "tornado" in the brain, beyond normal human experience. Finally recognizing that it was a demonic attack, he commended himself to the Virgin Mary, commanded the demons to leave, and sprinkled holy water on himself. It instantly abated.

Fr. Chad Ripperger, a seasoned exorcist, estimated that 25 percent of Americans suffer from demonic obsessions.[33] He said that people, by their sinful behaviors of the mind, are opening themselves to evil—although, at times, Satan targets people to attack, such as exorcists, as part of his regular harassment of their ministry.

---

[33] Fr. Chad Ripperger, "Conference on Exorcisms," *Sensus Traditionis*, 2019, posted on Virgo Potens, October 15, 2019, https://virgopotens .org/blog/2019/10/11/xol3hgznlfzud9synqc8m3aw2f6bhn.

How do we know if the thoughts in our minds are simply our human weakness or directly demonic? Demonic obsessions can be unusually intense and powerful; they are out of proportion to the reality of our lives; and they may lessen or even abate with prayer.

To protect ourselves, we ought to focus our thoughts on good and holy things. We must steer clear of using our minds for evil or sinful behaviors. And, if we find our minds bombarded with obsessive, negative, and self-injurious thoughts, we should commend ourselves to God and pray.

Exorcist Diary 59

Possession as a Grace?

To be possessed sounds like a disaster. God knows, it is a very ugly affair. I never say the word *possessed* when diagnosing someone. In the past, if we told people they were possessed, they were devastated; some started to cry. I understand. Now I simply tell them they have some evil spirits and need to have Jesus cast them out.

But the reality is this: being possessed can be an occasion for an incredible grace! Many who are possessed have been mired in sin. Others have been cursed or traumatized, or both. They have demons seriously infecting their lives in very negative ways. They are carrying evil burdens. Still others have been tormented for years, physically or mentally, or both, with medical and other healing sciences unable to find the cause. These afflicted people need help. They need Jesus and His healing grace.

When they are finally liberated, the formerly possessed are often in the first pews of the Church. They know the truth. They know how evil Satan is. They know that God cares and has freed them. In the course of their exorcisms, they went through an extensive and very personal catechesis.

I wouldn't wish possession on anyone. But I have witnessed great graces as a result. For many, the experience led them out of their spiritual Hell and into the saving arms of Jesus.

Theological Reflection

Healing versus Symptom Relief

When people come to an exorcist, they are almost always suffering from a variety of negative symptoms. These can be unexplained physical maladies, intense negative mental obsessions, or strong adverse reactions to sacred things. Understandably, they come to the exorcist hoping he will say a prayer and rid them of these torturous afflictions.

Exorcisms can indeed alleviate demonic symptoms. But these afflictions usually indicate the need for a deeper healing of the person's psyche and spirit. In addition to the powerful prayers of the Church, the exorcist will typically prescribe a healing regimen tailored to the specific needs of the individual.

He may also ask the person to see a professional counselor and address any underlying issues of trauma or abuse. He may suggest a series of spiritual sessions to bring healing to specific spiritual wounds. He will always insist on the individual's living an intense life of prayer and virtue, including regular reception of the sacraments of Penance and the Eucharist.

Without this deeper regimen of inner healing, exorcism prayers will likely have limited or no efficacy. Many request an exorcism because they want symptom relief, but fewer are willing to walk the more difficult path of healing and holiness. Those few who decide to deepen their spiritual lives find that their demonic afflictions are actually a source of grace, as those afflictions lead them into a dynamic relationship of gratitude and peace with the one Source of all healing.

Exorcist Diary 60

Demons Sending More Texts

I received some more snarky texts from demons. They were gloating over a possessed person and texted me: "She is mine, she has been handed over. There is nothing you can do." I responded, "The Blessed Virgin Mary can." I texted an Ave Maria, and they responded: "No, Rossetti!" The Virgin must have interceded.

I then texted: "Vade, Satanas" (meaning "Leave, Satan"), and they responded, "We will not." Then they taunted me, "Do you see what happens?" They were referring to their threatening to attack the possessed soul to try to get me to stop praying. I ignored it and kept texting prayers.

I am happy to get texts from demons. At that moment, they are no longer hiding and are exposed. We can then focus prayers directly on them. It weakens the demons and helps to free the afflicted person faster.

When demons are exposed, they quickly lose the battle. You would think they would refrain from sending these exposing texts, but they can't help it. They are so narcissistic and arrogant that they can't stop. They compulsively posture, threaten, and boast. But it is all empty bluster.

All I can say is, "Send more texts!" Our little team will respond with prayers.

Exorcist Diary 61

An Infested House

We received a call from a fireman who said his house had a problem. Shortly after the family had moved in, many strange things began to happen. Lights turned off and on mysteriously; doors unlocked by themselves; Alexa started to play music without being prompted; one of the rooms became abnormally frigid; and there was a red light in a hallway where no light could penetrate.

Moreover, he and his wife saw a dark menacing figure several times. It turns out that the house had previously been used for drug and sex trafficking, and several people had been killed there in a shootout.

When houses are infested with demons, it is typically the result of sinful behaviors done in the building. As I've noted, unnatural deaths in a place, such as abortions, are especially strong openings for the demonic. Conducting occult rituals is also a huge open door for a demonic infestation. After such evils, demons may claim the place as theirs and threaten those who try to expel them.

The remedy is to exorcise the house. The owners should liberally use sacramentals, including crucifixes and holy water, and pray the Rosary and deliverance prayers. A deeply entrenched demonic presence, however, may require the ministry of a priest.

In such cases, he will want permission to use the Church's ritual for exorcising a place, and he may want to say Masses of reparation there.

Jesus always wins. But sometimes it takes a bit of perseverance before a place is totally cleansed.

Demons or Ghosts?

The Catholic Church has not spoken authoritatively about the existence of ghosts. The faithful are welcome to believe in them or not. But ghosts, if they exist, are different from demons. Ghosts are reportedly the spirits of deceased human beings, and demons are fallen angels.

Ghosts and demons act differently. Ghosts are trying to get people's attention because they need prayers to go to their final place of rest. But demons are only out to control, terrorize, and destroy. So, one sign that there are demons in a place is that they do destructive things, such as breaking objects and attacking people. Ghosts harmlessly manipulate objects and such to get people's attention, although people are naturally frightened.

When people claim to have ghosts in their houses, they are often mistaken, and in reality, they have demons. Demons will sometimes pretend to be friendly ghosts in order to develop a relationship with the family and worm their way into their lives. Only after they have firmly established themselves does it become apparent that they are demons and thus are much harder to exorcise.

If you believe you have ghosts, then prayers for the dead are in order. Having Masses said for the deceased souls is most efficacious. In cases of intense hauntings, it is best if a priest can say one or more Masses in the room of the house that is the center of the troubles.

When demons are present, prayers of deliverance and exorcism are needed. Prayers and Masses of reparation for the evil that invited the demons into the place can be helpful as well.

Exorcist Diary 62

In the Midst of a Demonic Onslaught

The demons have now launched a full-out attack against Jason (see entry 42). They are sending manipulative and accusatory texts. (A friend walked into Jason's room and saw his phone sitting face up and the keys typing messages by themselves.) The demons are intensely tormenting him, nightly burning crosses into his body and more. They are getting into his and his family's heads, inflaming their frustration, anger, and despair.

In the texts, the demons continue to boast: "He is ours." "You will tire of this and give up." "We will drag him to Hell." "You will never defeat us."

But if you listen closely, you will hear that it is really the demons who are despairing. They fear giving up. They are insisting that Jason belongs to them because they know they are losing him. It is just one piece of a cosmic battle that they have already lost on Calvary. Their lot is one of defeat and despair.

Our task is to support Jason and his family, who are suffering terribly. Their anger, frustration, and feelings of hopelessness are very real. This is the challenge of an intense exorcism: keeping the team together and moving forward in the middle of a demonic onslaught.

We have engaged our prayer warriors. We need their prayers. I speak to Jason and his family about trusting in Jesus. I tell them this trial will end. The demons will be cast out. They must persevere.

I worry. I stay close to them during this trial. I tell them that we will never abandon them. Neither will Jesus. And I pray:

Remember, O most gracious Virgin Mary, that never was it known that anyone who fled to thy protection, implored thy help, or sought thy intercession was left unaided . . .

Exorcist Diary 63

"I Have No Legs"

Demons are cowards—despite all their bluster and arrogance. They like to hide, and part of our ministry is to flush them out. Then we invoke the holy name of Jesus to cast them out.

In one session, I commanded them, "In the name of Jesus, stop hiding. Stand up and face the light."

The response, "I cannot."

"Why not?" I demanded.

"I have no legs."

I said, "You know what I mean."

It is true that demons have no legs. As spiritual beings, they have no bodies. But the possessed, and others, will sometimes see them as dark, shadowy figures. They seem to be floating. They are often hooded, and their grotesque faces are not seen. They, indeed, have no legs.

Demons tend to be literalists. But when this one said, "I have no legs," I think it was a little demonic sarcasm. The fact remains that they are cowards and hide in the dark.

Jesus is the Light of the World. All the darkness and evil are cast out when the light of Christ shines. I often lay my hands on the afflicted and pray that the light of Christ will shine throughout every cell of their being and cast out the darkness.

Theological Reflection

Demons Hide

Demons' best defense is hiding and deception. They are most successful when they can entice people to sin and to do evil without even being aware of the demons' presence. Satan and his demons are especially effective in today's world because many do not believe in their existence or their activity in our world. While we cannot blame Satan for all the evil in this world, his footprints are everywhere.

The demons especially try to hide during an exorcism, particularly in the initial sessions when we are trying to determine whether the person's problems are psychological or spiritual. They will try to convince everyone, including the afflicted person, that it is all psychological. Many of the symptoms they provoke mimic psychological diagnoses.

The demons know that if their presence is discovered and a priest exorcist prays the Church's Rite of Exorcism, they will be in big trouble. They are no match for a straight-up fight with Jesus and His Church, which is what the priest represents and invokes. So they do everything they can to hide.

The good news for exorcists is that demons can usually hide for only a limited time after the prayers begin. Imagine someone trying to hide undetected in a closet. But then throw gasoline on the person and light it. Yikes!

The person may try to remain silent but will quickly start to scream.

To flush demons out, we use sacramentals such as holy water and a crucifix. Most importantly, we will say deliverance prayers invoking the grace of God and the holy name of Jesus. Many times, I will directly command the demons, "In the holy name of Jesus Christ, I command you to manifest." I say this prayer in a foreign language so the afflicted person does not know what I am saying, but the demons certainly do!

Demons are incredibly tough and can last for quite a while before they start to react to the prayers. I typically find that they may last for twenty to thirty minutes but then will manifest, if they are present. I have had one of the strongest demons, Beelzebul, not manifest for an hour and a half. But even he, one of the strongest "lieutenants" in Hell, eventually began to writhe and manifest his suffering.

When the demons do manifest, the afflicted person's body will start to react visibly. There are common symptoms. The body will convulse; the eyes may roll back; the person may flail and start to scream. With each case, the symptoms may be somewhat different. But the key is to pray so that any demons present will manifest and then to be alert to these symptoms and to discern their origin, whether spiritual or psychological.

Exorcist Diary 64

Satan Unleashed

God usually keeps Satan on a tight leash. His power and actions are limited. In this day and age, however, it appears that the prince of this world has been almost completely unleashed. It used to be that Satan did his evil in a hidden way. Now it is open warfare.

Holy statues are pulled down; sacred images are desecrated. Religion is mocked, and God's laws are rejected. One of the strongest signs of Satan's presence is a hatred for the Catholic Church. Churches are burned around the world.

Another strong sign of Satan's presence is discord, violence, and death. We see these everywhere. The increasing civil discord in this country has erupted into open conflict.

Some weeks ago, one of our specially gifted persons said, "The demonic is way more active than before; their activity is more pronounced, and they have less fear than normal.... Their 'limit' seems to be nonexistent lately; their violent actions have been increasingly daring and brutal." She said this several months ago. It has come to the fore now with a vengeance.

It is time for us to take up our own weapons. One of our most powerful weapons is the Rosary. We pray it daily to cast out Satan and to invoke the aid of the Blessed Mother. Another weapon is a pious reception of Holy Communion. We offer Jesus' presence in the Eucharist for this country and for the world. Finally, we might say deliverance prayers daily—especially priests in an exercise of their spiritual authority.

Jesus has won the battle. But how many poor souls will be lost in these terrible days? Pray, pray, pray for the conversion of sinners and that Satan will once again be tightly leashed.

Exorcist Diary 65

The Battle Rages

A seasoned exorcist called me and said he was recently doing a session and commanded the demon to reveal its name. (Knowing the name gives the exorcist more power over the demon.) The demon, through the mouth of the possessed person, said with a mocking sneer, "You know who I am. I am Gressil. I am going to get you!"

Indeed, he had encountered this vicious, high-ranking demon a few years ago and had cast him out. He responded, "I have Jesus. And the same thing will happen to you again. You will be cast out in Jesus' name."

For the next two days, he was subjected to intense demonic obsessions. He endured these with faith and reached out to a fellow priest for prayer. The priest prayed over him, and he is fine.

This exemplary priest gave us an example for these challenging times. He faced the demon's threat with courage. He responded in faith that Jesus is Lord and casts out the strongest of demons. He endured his sufferings as a sacrifice that God was asking of his priestly ministry. He humbly asked for assistance.

We, too, should face the struggles and evils of our day with faith in Jesus. We, too, should embrace our sufferings, uniting them to Jesus' Cross. And, if needed, we should reach out for help from others. In Jesus, we, too, will triumph.

Exorcist Diary 66

Who Is the "Terror of Demons"?

At the beginning of a session, I typically ask the afflicted person if he or she has a devotion to a particular saint. If so, we will invoke that saint during the prayers. Recently, in response to my query, a person said, "St. Joseph."

So, during the session, while the demons were fully manifesting, I invoked St. Joseph. The demons frantically yelled, "No. Not him. Stop!" Pressing the advantage, our team prayed again and again and again, "St. Joseph, pray for us. St. Joseph cast out the demons." This afflicted person has made considerable progress in recent days and her life is almost back to normal, with few demonic symptoms.

Many people think of St. Joseph as a kind, pious old man who cared for Jesus and Mary. This is true. But he is a true father figure—strong in faith and a defender of the family. Venerable Mother Mary of Agreda (1602–1665), in her famous work, *The Mystical City of God*, said that God granted St. Joseph certain privileges, including "inspiring the demons with terror at the mere mention of his name."[34]

---

[34] Venerable Mary of Agreda, "The Happy Death of St. Joseph," in *The Mystical City of God*, posted on EWTN, https://www.ewtn.com/catholicism/library/happy-death-of-saint-joseph-5426.

In the Litany of St. Joseph, he is invoked under many titles, most notably "terror of demons." As Fr. Donald Calloway, author of *Consecration to St. Joseph*, notes: "After the Virgin Mary, demons fear St. Joseph more than any other saint."[35] Blessed Bartolo Longo, a satanic priest before his conversion, told us: "It is a great blessing for souls to be under the protection of the saint [Joseph] whose name makes demons tremble and flee."[36]

You can find the following prayer in Fr. Calloway's *Consecration to St. Joseph*:

Prayer to St. Joseph, Terror of Demons

Saint Joseph, Terror of Demons, cast your solemn gaze upon the devil and all his minions, and protect us with your mighty staff. You fled through the night to avoid the devil's wicked designs; now with the power of God, smite the demons as they flee from you! Grant special protection, we pray, for children, fathers, families, and the dying. By God's grace, no demon dares approach while you are near, so we beg of you, always be near to us! Amen.

---

[35] Fr. Donald H. Calloway, M.I.C., "St. Joseph: Terror of Demons," *Signs and Wonders for Our Times*, April 24, 2020, https://sign.org/articles/st-joseph-terror-of-demons-187491.

[36] Ibid.

Exorcist Diary 67

Pagan Gods as Demons

We have encountered demons identified with pagan gods. Invoking such non-Christian "deities" may actually be invoking Satan and his minions, whether intended or not.

In the midst of a session, one of the highest-ranking demons was forced to reveal his name: Baal. That name is associated with a Canaanite deity sometimes identified as the god of fertility or rain. Sacral sexual intercourse by pagan priests and priestesses and sexual promiscuity are associated with Baal worship.

So we wrapped a priest's cincture (the white cord that symbolizes chastity and purity and is worn around the priest's waist for Mass) around the afflicted person's waist and commanded the demon to leave. Baal screamed, "Take it off! Take it off!" The demon of sexual promiscuity was tortured by it. Shortly thereafter, by the power of Jesus, he was cast out.

The sexual promiscuity of today reveals that Baal worship is very much alive, whether we realize it or not. The antidote is pure, chaste living, which quickly casts out even the highest-ranking demons.

Exorcist Diary 68

A Horror beyond Description

I was doing a preliminary interview with a person who reported seeing dark, shadowy figures. This is a sign that the person may truly be tormented by demons. In lower levels of demonic possession or oppression, demons are typically hooded and their faces are not seen. If the person enters more deeply into a relationship with the demons, and thus more inured to evil, the horrible visage of demons becomes increasingly revealed.

One possessed person had a direct vision of demons that he described to me. He said, "The demons were horrific to look at. They were distorted and misshapen.... Some had claws instead of hands.... If they had two eyes or any recognizable limbs, they were malformed.... These demons were all like naked, ugly, vicious animals." He went on to say that they were uglier than one could possibly imagine. He added that horror movies do not even come close.

Should one end up in Hell, Satan and his demons are completely revealed. St. Faustina said the sixth major torture of Hell is "the constant company of Satan." She exclaimed, "How terribly ugly Satan is! Just the sight of him is more disgusting than all the torments of Hell."[37] Similarly, St. Catherine of Siena, in her famous book, the *Dialogues*, said, "The sight [of the devil] is more painful to them, because they see him in his own form, which is so horrible that the heart of man could not imagine it."[38]

St. Catherine also revealed that the "saints exult in the sight of [God], refreshing themselves with joyousness ... with such abundance of love."[39]

This will be our end, either the joyous sight of the surpassing beauty of love that is God, or the indescribable hideousness that is Satan—forever.

---

[37] *Diary*, no. 540.
[38] *The Dialogue of St. Catherine of Siena* (London: Kegan Paul, Trench, Trubner, 1907), no. 22, Catholic Treasury, http://www.catholictreasury.info/books/dialogue/diag33.php.
[39] Ibid.

Exorcist Diary 69

The Stench of Evil

One of our priests was detained and arrived late for the exorcism. He leaned over and said, "I smell an awful stench." He did not smell it with his physical senses. It was a grace, albeit a rather ugly grace, for him to sense the presence of evil as an ugly stench.

Some time ago, one of our possessed souls had a vision of Hell, and he told us, "Fire engulfed all of the bodies of the souls, the smell of rotting flesh and melting skin was atrocious; it made me want to throw up."

In her *Dialogues*, St. Catherine of Siena relayed what God told her, "The stain of Adam's sin ... corrupted the whole human race and gave out a stench."[40] Sin and evil have the horrible stench of death.

On the other hand, whenever the saints appear to souls, there is often a beautiful smell. Whenever Padre Pio has appeared, in his earthly life or later from Heaven, people often describe the sweet scent of roses, violets, or lilies. The presence of St. Thérèse of Lisieux is associated with the scent of roses. Such is the odor of sanctity, or, more technically, osmogenesia.

---

[40] Ibid., no. 8, http://www.catholictreasury.info/books/dialogue/diag19.php.

Heaven will be a feast both for the soul and the resurrected body, including the beautiful scents of holiness. Hell is so vile that souls will want to retch.

Exorcist Diary 70

Bishops in Hell

We were exorcising a young religious woman. She became possessed not through her own fault but through the evil done by her family. Not fair? You bet it's not fair. But as your mother told you long ago, "Life is not fair."

In the course of this woman's liberation, the demons did everything they could to dissuade her from staying in religious life. I recall a story about the saintly Curé of Ars, St. John Vianney. At one point, Satan told him, "If there were three like you on this earth, my kingdom would be destroyed." One faithful religious can do immense damage to Satan's kingdom.

So, the prince of darkness is eager to destroy this woman's religious vocation. On at least three occasions over a year of prayer sessions, she picked up her head and said in great dismay, "I see many, many bishops in Hell!" To discourage this young religious, Lucifer was showing her a sea of bishops in Hell. Lucifer is a most cunning tempter.

Yes, of course, there is likely to be a number of bishops in Hell. However, my experience is that the vast majority of bishops are kind, pious men who spend themselves in God's service. But Satan did not show her those.

Theological Reflection

Upon Death, Do Possessed People Go to Hell?

In the course of an exorcism, demons will taunt afflicted people with condemning and ugly messages. One consistent demonic message is that God doesn't care about them and that when they die, the demons will drag them to Hell. I have had several possessed people ask, "If I die still possessed, will I go to Hell?"

Being possessed is not a judgment on one's spiritual state. This sounds strange. But it is true. There are more than a few possessed people who became possessed not due to any fault of their own. Innocent people can be cursed by others. Children can be dedicated to demons by their parents. While many people become possessed by their own evil actions, others are innocent victims.

There have even been great saints who were possessed for a time by demons. One who stands out is St. Mary of Jesus Crucified, the "little Arab." Born in Palestine, Mariam Baouardy became a Carmelite sister and was favored with many mystical experiences. She was also tormented by demons and possessed at least twice as a spiritual trial.

Though most possessed people are not victim souls like St. Mary of Jesus Crucified, the experience of being possessed can become a true source of grace and conversion. The afflicted comes to know firsthand the reality of evil and the saving power of Jesus.

Like all experiences in life, demonic possession can become a grace. As Scripture says, "All things work for good for those who love God" (Rom. 8:28).

Exorcist Diary 71

A Wounded Beast

Jason (see entry 62) woke up with several long, ugly, eighteen-inch gouges on his back. It looked as if a beast had raked its claws down his back. In fact, that's exactly what happened.

The demons' attacks against him have intensified. He is aggressively assaulted and abused. At night, and even during the day, his bed shakes violently when he lies on it. Jason is terrified. Friends freak out when they see it.

In our latest session, Jason said his eyes were burning when he looked at the crucifix. He cried, "My eyes are on fire!" Several times, he was choked to the point of passing out. He relayed to me that the demons were demanding that I take off my stole during the session. The sight of my priestly stole, too, causes much suffering. Of course, I refuse.

Jason's mother is distraught. She complains, "The situation is getting worse. The demons are getting stronger!" And Jason, because of the physical possession, feels much of the demons' pain. He is suffering greatly.

The demons themselves are suffering intensely and are actually getting weaker. The stole, the crucifix, and other sacramentals are torturing them. The Rite of Exorcism is loosening their grip, and they are fighting back like a dying animal. Like a mortally wounded beast, they are thrashing and lashing out.

It cuts to the heart to see Jason suffer so much. I wish there were an easier way, and I tell him so. These are dark moments that push Jason and his family to the limit. I trust that God will not allow the demons to push them beyond what they can stand.

I encourage them to pray, "Jesus, I trust in You." It is my prayer as well.

Indigestion or Demons?

We began tonight's exorcism session, and within about twenty minutes, the afflicted person said her stomach started to hurt. She normally does not have stomach problems. I gave her a little cup with some exorcised olive oil to drink. She had quite a reaction and said it burned all the way down. Then her stomach pain went away. I have had energumens ingest exorcised oil before, and some have immediately retched, perhaps vomiting up some evil.

Demons often attack the head or the stomach, or both, especially when they are cornered and suffering due to the exorcism prayers. Humans are particularly vulnerable in both places, and the demons exploit our weaknesses. These demonic effects are temporary and typically not severe, but they can be distressing.

One of the ways our gifted team members know that demons are present is that they themselves quickly get a headache and a feeling of nausea when the afflicted person enters the room; the stronger the demonic presence, the stronger the symptoms. In really bad cases, the gifted person can hardly stand being in the same room.

We have to be careful with physical symptoms; our default is to assume a natural cause, and thus we engage a natural treatment. But sometimes it is obvious that the cause is preternatural.

Exorcist Diary 73

Narcissism Is Hell

When reading at Mass, I had always wondered how to pronounce the name of the Canaanite deity (who is really a demon) called Baal. In a subsequent exorcism session, I found out!

We were in a rough case, and we knew it would be a long, ugly battle. At one point, I demanded to know, "How many demons are present?" The snarky demonic response: "Too many for you!" As the demonic cohort got weaker, I was able to force them to reveal the total number of demons present — 856. That's a lot of demons! Then I demanded to know the names of the leaders, and the names given in response sounded like a "who's who" in Hell. This was not going to be easy.

As the months passed, one by one the leaders and their minions were cast out in Jesus' name. At one point, we got to Baal. He was forced to reveal that there were 679 demons remaining. We priest exorcists again started praying the Rite, and as always, the demons howled in agony. They were so weak at this point that the holy water scalded them, and the mere sight of the crucifix was agonizing. Everything tortured them.

I commanded Baal to leave and pronounced his name, Ba'al, with two syllables. To my surprise, he firmly corrected me: "It is Baal," and he pronounced it with one syllable. Later in the

215

session, he again corrected me and said his name was pronounced Baal (like the bleat of a sheep with an *l* on the end).

This was bizarre. There we were in the midst of a pitched battle, and he was screaming his lungs out and about to be cast back into Hell. And yet he was focused on how to pronounce his name. This was narcissism beyond belief!

Demons are complete narcissists, and Satan is the biggest narcissist of all. In Hell, no one thinks of another's good. It is pure self-focus and, as with Baal, the bizarre, irrational thinking of an intellect succumbed to evil. Satan would sacrifice every demon under him in Hell just for his own pleasure.

This makes the infinitely generous self-sacrifice of God in Jesus all the more striking. Satan would skewer us for his own benefit. The heart of Jesus was pierced on the Cross for our salvation. Something to think about.

Exorcist Diary 74

Are Demons Brilliant or Stupid?

In the midst of exorcism sessions, it is clear how much disdain demons have for humans. Their innate angelic intelligence and the power given to them—as part of their nature—are much greater than ours. These natural powers were retained in the fall. They see themselves as superior to us, and, by nature, this is true. Seeing such intense and wicked disdain in the possessed person's eyes helps us discern a demonic presence.

But demons are deprived of the God-given grace of wisdom. Sometimes they act like immature, adolescent gang members, especially the lower-ranking demons. Also, their natural reason is corrupted by their being permeated by evil. They are like supercomputers with completely corrupted software; their thoughts are twisted and perverted. Satan and his followers are particularly good at tempting and manipulating. Their perverted intellects make them masters only of evil.

Does this make a difference to us? Yes! As Pope Francis has said time and again, "Don't argue or fight directly with Satan." Whenever accosted by evil, we turn to Jesus to fight for us.

The demons are always dissing me. For example, they often say, "You have no power over us." My response: "This is true. But Jesus does, and in His holy name, I command you to leave!"

As an exorcist, I need to be especially careful of Satan's hidden manipulations. Behind the scenes, this master of evil is working subtly to snare us in his hidden traps. Thus, we need to pray much and listen to the Holy Spirit, who unmasks Satan's evil plans and guides us safely through.

Exorcist Diary 75

Can You Convert Demons?

I recently heard of a group—perhaps it was just a bad rumor—that invited demons into their bodies in order to convert them. Yikes! What a bad move!

I was in the midst of an exorcism recently, and the demons were suffering greatly as a result of the prayers. I commanded them to answer, "Did you make a bad choice rejecting God?"

The answer came back reluctantly: "Yes."

I then asked, "Are you suffering because of it?"

Again the reluctant response: "Yes."

I concluded with the question "So would you change your choice if you could?"

They answered, "No."

(This exchange was part of the exorcism itself, that is, commanding the demons to admit the truth and face the evil they had chosen. It caused them great distress.)

Incredible! This is an example of the sickness of evil and sin. Demons know they made a bad choice but still wouldn't change it.

Demons cannot be converted. So I say to all those in deliverance ministry: don't try. Don't try to convince demons of the truth. You are wasting your breath and could likely open yourself to their subtle manipulations and deceits.

At times, however, I will force them to tell the truth. For example, I will command them through the power of Christ to answer, "Whose death and Resurrection smashed Satan's king-dom?" They will respond only under duress, "Jesus'."

In an exorcism, we "pour the Truth down their throats," as one senior exorcist described the Rite, but we cannot convert them. They are lost forever.

Theological Reflection

The Choice of the Angels Is Immutable

When one wants to speak theologically about angels and demons, the best place to start is with the Angelic Doctor, St. Thomas Aquinas. He wrote that a beatified angel (an angel who did not fall but enjoys the ultimate beatitude in God) can no longer sin. He added, "From its perfect union with the uncreated good, such as is the union of beatitude, it is rendered unable to sin."[41]

Similarly, St. Thomas said that Satan and the fallen angels "are not capable of repenting, [they] cling immovably to sin."[42] This is affirmed in the *Catechism*: "There is no repentance for the angels after their fall" (no. 393).

Angels learn differently from humans. We learn slowly, by reason and by experience. At the moment of their choice, the angels were given a full awareness of the choice before them and its complete ramifications. They were given a direct apprehension of the truth, and yet they still rejected God.

This was demonstrated experientially in the previous diary entry, "Can You Convert Demons?" The demons were asked if they had made a bad choice in rejecting God and were suffering as a result. They admitted that this was true. Yet they said that, if given the choice again, they would not change their minds. They are

[41] *ST*, I, q. 62, art. 8.
[42] *ST*, I, q. 64, art. 2.

confirmed forever in their evil choice and their hatred of God.

This is the mystery of evil (2 Thess. 2:7). But is it any less of an insanity for us humans? What could be more irrational than to reject the source of all love and all goodness, God, and to choose Satan and his evil ways?

Exorcist Diary 76

Don't Feed the Demons

We always have a few cases that seem to go too slowly or stall out. The team faithfully prays with the afflicted person, but progress seems virtually nil. Then we know it's time to discern: What are the demons feeding on?

Demons especially thrive on anger, unforgiveness, arrogance, and disobedience. As long as these are festering in the afflicted person's heart, the demons are not going to leave. So we take the person through a spiritual healing process to address these issues. The person needs to let go and allow Jesus to heal his or her wounds.

Recently, I have found other wounds that stall our progress, such as self-deprecation and pervasive fear. One afflicted person hates himself; the demons are using that as a doorway to enter and latch on like parasites. A second person is full of fear, and she becomes overly distressed at the least change or uncertainty; whenever this happens, she regresses, and it seems as if we have to start all over again. Both of these cases were referred to a Catholic psychotherapist to aid in healing these wounds.

If you feed demons, they won't leave. In an exorcism, we must discern and withdraw from demons any sustenance they are getting. That will starve them out. Finally, they will get so weak that they will leave.

I suspect that this is true in all of our lives. It might be good to take a moment and reflect: Are there any wounds in us that feed the evil one? May Jesus heal us all!

Exorcist Diary 77

Hell as God's Mercy?

It always amazes me how much the demons suffer during an exorcism. After fifteen to twenty minutes, even the stoutest of demons start screaming. Spray a little holy water on them, hold up a crucifix, or say the Rite of Exorcism, and they scream. The pain is so intense that, if they were mortal, it would kill them on the spot.

Some exorcists believe that the pain of an exorcism is, for demons, greater than the pain of Hell. They can suffer it for a short time, but eventually they cannot endure it, and they leave. It often makes me wonder, "If demons cannot stand the sight of a wooden cross or a little holy water, what would a direct vision of God be like for them?" It would be a cruel suffering beyond imagining.

Pope St. Leo the Great said something similar about damned souls: "For the eye that is unclean would not be able to see the brightness of the true light, and what would be happiness to clear minds would be a torment to those that are defiled.[43] For fallen souls, as for demons, seeing God in Heaven and experiencing holy things would be an insufferable torment.

[43] Sermon 95, 8–9; *PL* 54, 465–466.

Hell is a terrible reality. I personally believe the gruesome visions of Hell of such mystics as St. Catherine of Siena, the children of Fatima, and St. Faustina. And yet, if the fallen angels and damned souls were put in the direct presence of the infinite holiness of God in Heaven, it is likely that their pain would be beyond insufferable.

This underscores the terrible destruction of the soul caused by sin. Holiness becomes a torment. Perhaps even the existence of Hell is yet another mercy of the Almighty.

Are There Many Who Are Saved?

The Catholic Church has never definitively weighed in on the question of how many souls will be saved. It is commonly believed that one-third of the angels fell; this is based upon an interpretation of Revelation 12:3–4: "It was a huge red dragon.... Its tail swept a third of the stars in the sky and hurled them down to the earth."

The best inkling we have of how many human souls will be saved can be found in the Gospel of Matthew: "The gate is wide and the road broad that leads to destruction, and those who enter through it are many. How narrow the gate and constricted the road that leads to life. And those who find it are few" (7:13–14).

Echoing this thought, St. Thomas wrote: "Since eternal happiness, consisting as it does in the vision of God, exceeds the common state of nature, and especially in so far as this is deprived of grace through the corruption of original sin, those who are saved are in the minority."[44]

Also, the Gospel of Luke tells us: "Much will be required of the person entrusted with much, and still more will be demanded of the person entrusted with more" (12:48). Bishops and priests should take this as a

[44] *ST*, I, q. 23, art. 8.

clear warning. Sadly, it is reasonable to assume that more than a few bishops and priests are in Hell (see entry 70).

No doubt Satan takes particular sadistic pleasure in the presence of these anointed souls in Hell since they remain sacramentally configured to Christ. Thus, Satan likely sees their hellish torture as a way to revenge himself on Jesus Christ, who destroyed his kingdom. He will likely use their damnation, if he can, to scandalize the faithful.

Exorcist Diary 78

A Taste of Hell

We were discerning with a young woman and her family whether she was possessed. She had a long history of dabbling in the occult, and she was starting to show a real aversion to anything of God.

When she came in for the first time, she was angry, agitated, and defiant. She spoke a lot of negative nonsense about God and said that Satan was stronger than Jesus. No amount of reason could sway her. But then we started to pray over her. At the end of the extended session, she became a quiet, gentle soul who expressed her gratitude. She was at peace.

Clearly, her initial angry, defiant rejection of God was a sign of her demonic possession. She spouted the lies of Satan and thus suffered from "demon brain" (see entry 26). As the demons' presence was weakened by the exorcism, she began to think and speak like a rational, loving human being.

There are many signs that indicate that someone is possessed. One sign is the presence of demonic traits or a foretaste of Hell, especially when the person is manifesting in the midst of an exorcism. During such manifestations, we often witness a snarky arrogance, a look of rage, and a narcissistic self-focus.

We read in her *Dialogues* the Lord told St. Catherine of Siena that, already in this life, the one who has chosen God tastes the "earnest of Heaven" and the one who chooses Satan "tastes the earnest of Hell."[45] Heaven or Hell already begin to show in our lives based on our lives and the choices we have made.

The more Satan is in our lives, the more we become angry, isolated, self-centered, and disobedient, and the more we feel victimized and blame God and everyone else for our misery. Satan promises his followers a great life, but, like all of his promises, it is a lie. He will make a soul miserable in this life and torment souls beyond description in the next.

The more God and Jesus are in our lives, the more we begin to realize His promise of joy and peace. Gratitude slowly fills the hearts of the faithful. For my part, I am continually confirmed in my faith when I see the awful wages of sin and evil, even in this life, contrasted with the joy that only God can give.

I go to bed each night thanking God for His presence in my life. It is our ministry to help return souls to God's peace, through the holy name of Jesus. I go to bed thanking God for this beautiful ministry as well.

[45] *The Dialogue of Saint Catherine of Siena*, chap. 54.

Satan's Rage Is Spreading

The look of Satan's rage is unmistakable. There are several traditional signs that a person is possessed: understanding or speaking
unknown languages, aversion to the sacred, occult knowledge,
and superhuman strength. I would add another: a look of inhu-
man rage. When you see it on a possessed person's face for the
first time, it takes your breath away.

Today, as I look out across this country, I see the same fire of
Satan's rage. And it is spreading. Hatred, bitterness, violence, and
rancor are everywhere. People cannot civilly dialogue. Backbiting
and constant criticism are the norm. Everywhere there is anger
and hatred. Satan's rage is spreading.

There is only one antidote: Jesus said, "Love your enemies"
(Matt. 5:44). Reverend Martin Luther King Jr. told us, "Hate
cannot drive out hate; only love can do that." Only love, only
God, can drive out Satan and his hatred.

Love your enemies (see the theological reflection "Love Is
Not a Warm Feeling," following entry 80). Love Democrats and
Republicans. Love the rich and love the poor. Love people of all
colors. Love those who commit acts of terrorism and love the

police. Love abusers and criminals. Where there is love, there is God.

Time is short. The fire is raging. We need love to put that fire out now.

Exorcist Diary 80

Love Satan?

In the midst of an exorcism, I said to the demons, "In the name of Jesus Christ, I command you to tell me the truth. Does Satan love you? Tell the truth." The reluctant reply came through clenched teeth: "No." I responded, "Tell me the truth, does Jesus love you?" Again came the reluctant reply: "Yes." So I responded, "You made a rotten choice, didn't you?" Silence.

Part of an exorcism is forcing the demons to admit the truth, which is a searing torture for them. All sin promotes denials and rationalizations. For the demons, to admit their sin and the consequent punishment is "pure Hell" and hastens their departure.

Jesus still loves the demons, although He obviously rejects their evil choice and their evil behavior. As a just judge, God punishes them for their evil. But God never stops loving. God cannot hate; hate is Satan's work. God is radiant, infinite, and transforming love.

We, too, must love everyone, including our "enemies." In fact, the Christian has no enemies. I do not hate demons. If I did, I could never exorcise them because I would be in league with them. I am sorry for their horrible choice, for which they will pay for an eternity.

I do not pray for them or try to convert them. That is futile. But I do love them for the intrinsic beauty that once was theirs as God's creation and is still present in some hidden way.

> But I say to you, love your enemies, and pray for those who persecute you, that you may be children of your heavenly Father, for he makes his sun rise on the bad and the good, and causes rain to fall on the just and the unjust.... So be perfect, just as your heavenly Father is perfect. (Matt. 5:44–45, 48)

Theological Reflection

Love Is Not a Warm Feeling

It is hard for people to understand Jesus' command to love one's enemies. His example on the Cross should inspire us. Jesus loved those who put Him to death. He gave His life for everyone, including the ones who killed Him.

This does not mean that Jesus had "warm feelings" about those who did evil. At times, Jesus was angry at those who rejected Him. As Scripture tells us, He looked "around at them with anger and grieved at their hardness of heart" (Mark 3:5). Moreover, Jesus was filled with a righteous anger when He saw how people defamed God's Temple. So He fashioned a whip of cords and drove them out, overturning the money changers' tables (see Matt. 21:12).

As noted previously, loving and forgiving do not necessarily mean having warm feelings toward everyone. In our baptismal promises, we reject Satan and all his works. At times, we will be filled with a righteous anger toward these works and the works of all who do evil.

But cursing others, harboring hatred, wishing others evil—all these come from Satan. If we engage in such, we are promoting Satan's agenda, not God's. God is infinite love and compassion. Does loving our enemies, including demons, open us up to letting evil into our lives? Not at all. Rather, it is rage, hatred, and unforgiveness that are doors to the demonic.

Some time ago, I let go of my anger toward the demons. I no longer hate them. There is a great inner freedom and peace in letting go of all such hatred and judgmentalism, even toward demons.

I feel bad for the damned and for all who reject God. They will endure everlasting torment, not by the will of God, but by their own sinful choice. For God "wills everyone to be saved and come to knowledge of the truth" (1 Tim. 2:4).

Exorcist Diary 81

Demons' Voices in Our Head

Recently, I have been struck by Satan's exploiting our psychological weaknesses, particularly in demonic obsessions. He is a master at sensing our fears, our desires for control, cracks in our self-esteem, and our vain desires to be held in esteem by others. Then, when these flawed emotions surface, Satan exploits and exaggerates them.

Demonic obsessions are often recognizable by their unusual strength and debilitating power. What normally would be a typical human fear becomes a wild, out-of-control panic. What normally would be a typical human feeling of low self-esteem becomes a screeching voice of self-reproach and condemnation in one's head.

What often distinguishes a demonic obsession from more normal psychological weaknesses is the power and suddenness of the attack. It is akin to a gale-force storm arising suddenly in the brain.

If the person is already possessed, these human weaknesses can "feed the demons" and make it more difficult to exorcise them. This is why we often complement our spiritual remedies with trips to a Christian psychotherapist or sessions with a practitioner of other truly Christian healing remedies. As the possessed person finds deep inner healing from such psychological wounds, the demons slowly lose their grip on the person.

All of us have flaws in our psychological wholeness. Such are the sequelae of Original Sin. As we find greater inner healing, the voice of Satan in our heads decreases. Then we can more easily hear the beautiful voice of God and the holy angels.

Exorcist Diary 82

Cursed Objects

A woman recommended that I share her story. She and her family have been the sad victims of voodoo curses. As a result, the entire family has suffered greatly, despite persistent prayers.

Recently, a two-foot doll was placed near the family's office. They said security cameras recorded a large man, who seemed to be jumping around, placing the doll next to the building at around four o'clock in the morning. They believe it was a cursed voodoo doll.

When the office was opened the next day, an office worker kicked the doll into the street. When he kicked it, he said it felt as if "it was packed with hard rocks," and it hurt his feet. The following day, he became very sick. Also, his car axle broke.

Now they are having a priest pray over him, in addition to the medical care he is getting. Unfortunately, they should have disposed of it properly.[46]

We recommend that people do not touch cursed objects with their bare hands. Sometimes people become ill as a result.

[46] For instructions on how to dispose of cursed objects safely, see the app "Catholic Exorcism" under "Disposing of Cursed Objects." See also www.catholicexorcism.org.

Normally, the laity can dispose of these objects. They should sprinkle a cursed object with holy water, ask God to lift any curses, and dispose of it by destroying, burning, or burying it or throwing it into a body of water. The key is to destroy the object so that it no longer resembles what it was. At that point, any curses and attached demons depart.

Unfortunately, some particularly evil cursed objects carry related curses. If anyone tries to destroy such an object, a curse of retaliation becomes attached to that person. The team and I have seen this in our own practice when a layman properly disposed of a particularly evil object. After a forty-five-minute prayer session with an exorcist, however, the attached demons departed. It is better for a priest to destroy such particularly evil objects, since he has additional protections.

Objects can truly be cursed. What gives them their evil power is the practitioner's invoking the power of Satan, consciously or unconsciously. Why God allows such a thing we do not know. But the team and I know it is real because we ourselves have encountered this reality several times.

Exorcist Diary 83

Curses Are Real!

Like many Americans, when I first began this ministry years ago, I didn't think much about curses. They seemed to be a relic of pagan superstition. But Fr. Gabriele Amorth said that 90 percent of the possession cases he faced were the result of curses.[47]

Sometime later, I was riding a train to the suburbs of Rome on my way to Tre Fontane,[48] a Trappist Abbey and the place of St. Paul's beheading. Across the street is the site of a 1947 reported Marian apparition, Our Lady of the Revelation.[49] So, it is a wonderful one-day pilgrimage from Rome.

While on the train, a young man, looking rather deranged, approached me and asked for money. I responded by offering him some cookies (I usually respond to such requests by giving food).

He was enraged and stared at me for an uncomfortably long time and then walked away. I first thought nothing of it but,

---

[47] Getlen, "How an Exorcist Priest Came Face-to-Face with the Devil Himself."

[48] See "San Paolo alle Tre Fontane," Churches of Rome Wiki, https://romanchurches.fandom.com/wiki/San_Paolo_alle_Tre_Fontane.

[49] "The Virgin of Revelation at Tre Fontane 10 Years Before!," Missionaries of Divine Revelation, https://www.mdrevelation.org/the-virgin-of-revelation-at-tre-fontane-10-years-before/.

within seconds, I felt spiritually attacked. It was like a gale-force wind blowing chaos in my brain. "Wow," I thought, "What is this?" It was strange, sudden, powerful, and overwhelming.

Then, the inspired thought came: the man had cursed me. So, I laid both of my priestly hands on my head and prayed a deliverance prayer. Within seconds, the attack stopped completely and things returned to normal.

God has ways of teaching exorcists about their ministry. Curses are real. This man did not have any power of his own. Rather, people who curse derive their power from Satan, knowingly or unknowingly. Sadly, for that man, he was doing Satan's bidding.

The Scriptures are very clear: "Bless those who persecute [you], bless and do not curse them" (Rom. 12:14). We may never curse another person. Cursing others is the work of Satan. Rather, I pray for this man. May he come to know the joy and peace of salvation in Christ.

Theological Reflection

Lifting Curses

Jesus Christ is Lord! As the Son of God, the second Person of the Blessed Trinity, He has complete authority over all creation, in Heaven, on earth, and under the earth. Moreover, in His supreme act of love, He gave Himself on the Cross and smashed Satan's kingdom. Thus, He has complete authority over Satan.

Jesus gives this authority to His apostles and His Church. As a result, the Church has the authority to lift curses. The priest acts in the name of the Church (*in nomine ecclesiae*) and invokes this authority in his ministry. When the priest prays, it is the official Church praying.

There are no special rites or prayers given by the Church to lift curses. The Church has been silent about this aspect of the deliverance ministry. So the faithful are welcome to accept the reality of curses or to reject them. But for those who do believe in curses and desire to be freed from one, a simple prayer invoking the power of Christ to lift the curse is often sufficient.

Individuals have authority over their own bodies and thus can pray directly to have a curse over themselves lifted. If the curse is particularly difficult to lift, however, one might request the assistance of a priest.

Sometimes prayers to lift curses are immediately effective; the team and I have witnessed this a number of times. In other situations, it may take repeated efforts. Also, some actions on the part of the person who has been cursed may be necessary. So, when curses are not immediately effective, we will look for anything blocking the curse from being lifted or anything sealing it in place. It might require a longer process of purification and prayer.

Exorcist Diary 84

Insensitive Exorcists

A woman recently contacted me via e-mail about the insensitive behavior of her exorcist. I cringed when I read it. She said the exorcist "hits me in the face with holy water" which, unfortunately, triggered her already existing post-traumatic stress disorder. Also, in the midst of a session, the exorcist started to command Jezebel to leave. She added, "I don't know if he thinks he is hurting and abusing the demons with this behavior, but since I am the one who lives in this body, when he is calling for Jezebel to leave, it is so very hurtful to me."

I am guilty of such insensitive behavior as well. *Mea culpa.* We exorcists are not noted for our kind pastoral manner. On behalf of all of us, I apologize to her and to all of our clients whom we deal with in rather gruff and sometimes insensitive ways.

I suppose it goes a bit with the territory. Over these years of doing exorcisms, I have been repeatedly spit at in the face, knocked down and suffered a concussion, choked several times to the point of passing out (demons have a surprisingly strong grip), bitten and suffered teeth marks, cussed out innumerable times, threatened often, and punched and kicked; and my ritual books have been ripped, and holy objects have been thrown across the room. And if the session goes well, the afflicted person will scream, thrash uncontrollably, and vomit lots of white foam.

Though I go into each session with confidence in the Lord, and I know I am basically protected, it is still a battle. We have our strong helpers restrain the afflicted, but it is not a perfect system. Sometimes we are caught off guard. So, I walk in with caution, and my first goal is to keep everyone safe. But I sometimes forget that I have a wounded and frightened person in front of me. *Mea culpa.*

My encouraging light is Padre Pio. He personally battled demons and had the marks to prove it. He was gruff and accused of being insensitive. He was noted for practically yelling at those closest to him, particularly when they sinned or needed correction. If there is room in Heaven for such a man, I trust there is room for our band of flawed exorcists. *Mea maxima culpa!*

In our training sessions for exorcists, a strong module needs to be included on pastoral care and pastoral sensitivity. In recognition of the woman who courageously contacted me, we will certainly include this in the days to come.

Satan's Minions

A husband and wife have been harassed for over a year by a woman who practices witchcraft and the occult. Unfortunately, there was an indiscretion, and the woman gained spiritual access into their lives. Now the witch won't let go.

The woman sends them voluminous texts every day. They have changed their phone number more than two dozen times, and she immediately knows the new number and bombards them. Moreover, each time she texts, they block her number. But she immediately gets through to them using a new number. They have done this hundreds of times. Her occult knowledge and abilities are not humanly possible and are clearly derived through her demonic connection.

Considerable prayers and breaking of occult ties and curses have not yet freed them from her. Moreover, despite repeated requests, the police cannot or will not help.

This individual is one of Satan's minions—that is, she is a person who has given herself to Satan and does his bidding. Through this woman, Satan is attempting to destroy the couple psychologically and, over many months, has been wearing them down.

In another case, there was a specially gifted, holy woman whose life and ministry were, as admitted by the demons, "foiling their plans." One of Satan's minions began to stalk her and harass her in an effort to get her to stop her pious life and ministry. This minion, likewise, had occult knowledge, knowing many personal things about this holy woman's life. She was harassed and threatened for weeks. Eventually, the minion gave up and left.

It is very sad when we run into human beings who are minions of Satan. In these two cases, it appears that God did not allow them to do any more than harass and tempt. But the emotional devastation can be great, such as in the first case.

Will Satan reward his human minions for their servitude? No. Rather, he will use them and drain them in this life. Then, when their lives are over, he will torture them for an eternity for his own sadistic pleasure.

Our prayers are first for these people who are targeted by Satan through his minions. Should we also pray for the minions themselves? I choose to do so. No one is outside the possibility of salvation on this side of eternity. But I am not hopeful.

Exorcist Diary 86

Halloween Will Be Ugly

I am starting to prepare spiritually for All Hallows' Eve. No bags of candy. No costumes. No pumpkins. As every year, it will be ugly.

Many of our spiritual sensitives will get pummeled by demons. One year, our team decided to pray over one of our most gifted people throughout the night, trying to shield her from the demonic attacks she has suffered yearly. It didn't work. She got thrashed anyway. But she said she appreciated our efforts.

Several of our other sensitives will experience increased demonic harassment. Many of our clients who are possessed or severely oppressed will suffer more intensely throughout the night. The priest exorcists themselves will typically get bombarded with demonic obsessions and an internal battle.

There are times during the year when the demonic is more powerful than usual, and Halloween is at the top of the list. It is the demons' distortion of the great feast of All Saints on the following day. Moreover, Satan's human minions will join in and cast curses, spells, and all sorts of evil, which doesn't help.

I wonder about parents who dress up their children as devils or witches. Do they have any idea? I do not know about the spiritual effects of such Halloween practices on the general population. But on the possessed and on exorcism teams, the night will typically be a time of trial. Our little team will spend the evening in Eucharistic adoration, keeping vigil. We will await the dawn and the feast of All Saints.

Then we will celebrate the myriads of holy people who daily surround us and come to our aid. The radiance of divine light shining through them will cast out the darkness. Once again, there will be peace.

Theological Reflection

Magic versus Grace

It is thought that carving scary faces in pumpkins has its derivation in the superstition that such faces would scare away the evil spirits that roamed the earth on All Hallows' Eve. Likewise, nazars are symbols with large eyes, thought to protect their wearers from the curse of the evil eye.

Clearly, these are pagan superstitions that have no place in Christian practice. They highlight the difference between a Christian understanding of grace and pagan superstitions and magic.

Magic posits that if one performs special rituals properly, a spiritual power is elicited. Thus, there are books of magic spells and magic rituals. Similarly, nazars and other special symbols are thought to have their own power. Christians eschew such practices. If such pagan rituals have any power, it comes through one's invoking Satan, whether one realizes it or not.

Christianity, on the other hand, sees all power and grace coming from God. When we use symbols of our Faith, such as holy pictures and crucifixes, we do not believe such sacramentals have any inherent power. Rather, through their pious use, we are invoking God's blessing and protection. This is why any use of pagan superstition or magic rituals is an offense against God. Such practices are a direct violation of the first commandment, to acknowledge and worship the one true God.

Exorcist Diary 87

A Curse Lifted

A woman who had good reason to believe she had been cursed recently contacted me. We prayed over her and lifted the curse. Here is what she just wrote back:

> There was a curse put on me that created a significant barrier to my finding employment and negatively impacted both personal and professional relationships. Since we met for deliverance prayers, I have found an excellent job. Although estrangement from my family has not improved to any significant degree, I did go to visit my mother and one of my brothers and his children. The resolution I received was an acceptance that the years of generational indifference to one another is something that will change only through prayer. This resolution for me is reflected in the peace I now feel with this acceptance.
>
> Overall, almost immediately after our praying together, I can only describe that the presence of a "blocking influence" that I have felt for so long was gone. This trial has been an amazing journey.
>
> I would like to share my story with those who could benefit from understanding the difficulties I had obtaining

assistance. Understanding and education in matters related to deliverance are still new to most dioceses and nonexistent in most parishes. I think there are some clergy who could learn from hearing about my experiences.

So again, thank you. All praise and glory to God for allowing this trial to end.

It is encouraging to me and our entire team to receive such affirmation. It happens quite a bit. We just received another affirming e-mail in which the woman wrote, "Thank you! You all changed my life! I am so grateful!"

These notes are good reminders to me of what God in His goodness does for us. All thanks and gratitude go to Jesus, our Lord. It was in His holy name that the curses were lifted.

Exorcist Diary 88

Our Powerful Intercessors

In our little chapel, we have several dozen relics of the saints. Depending on the situation, we will bring a few out to use during each exorcism. One day, I had in hand a small, 1½-inch-diameter theca, or container, with a relic of St. Peter in it. I laid the theca on the temple of the afflicted person, and the body visibly jerked.

I commanded him to tell us which saint it was (keeping the theca's identity hidden), and he said, "Peter." Demons aren't psychic per se, but they know some things that are hidden to humans. Clearly, this relic was causing the demons considerable distress.

Another of our go-to saints is the young Italian mystic St. Gemma Galgani. We will often invoke her aid during exorcisms. Several times the afflicted have told me that they felt a special healing grace when we called upon her. We have similar stories about Padre Pio and other saintly intercessors.

One of the great graces we receive in our ministry is a personal experience of the truths of the Catholic Faith. In those sessions, we experienced firsthand the powerful Communion of Saints. These holy men and women are with us, helping us in our lives and ministries, including helping us cast out demons.

Let us echo the words of the abbot St. Bernard: "When I think of them, I feel myself inflamed by a tremendous yearning.... We long to share in the citizenship of Heaven, to dwell with the spirits of the blessed." May we, too, long to be counted among the saints and one day join their company.

Theological Reflection

Relics of the Saints

Starting with the early Church, the bodily remains of the martyrs and saints were venerated. Altars were erected over their tombs, and Masses were said on those altars. Perhaps the most notable is the great Basilica of St. Peter, erected over the tomb of St. Peter in the Vatican. In modern times, fixed altars have an altar stone in which the relic of a saint is deposited.

The saint's body itself is thought to be holy, and having it in one's possession is considered a blessing. For example, Venice has long prided itself on having the remains of St. Mark, which were taken from Alexandria in the ninth century by pious merchants and eventually enshrined in the Basilica of St. Mark. Having these remains is thought to bring a special grace and protection to the people and the city through the intercession of a powerful saint.

In modern times, relics of the saints, such as small pieces of bone, drops of dried blood, or pieces of hair, are preserved in small sealed containers. A common way of preserving these remains is to place them, as noted in the previous diary entry, in a small theca, sometimes about 1½ inches in diameter, although some are larger. This can then be placed in a larger reliquary for exposition.

These small pieces of the saint's body are called first-class relics. Second-class relics are pieces of a saint's clothing or something the saint used. Third-class relics are items touched to the saint's body or touched to a first-class relic.

Down through the centuries, many cures and miracles have been attributed to the faithful's touching these relics and invoking the intercession of the saints. Relics of the saints are considered to be sacramentals and are commonly used in exorcisms.

Exorcist Diary 89

Demons of Discord

During my night prayer, I experienced strong feelings of discord regarding other members of our team. It was out of proportion with the events. It didn't make sense. Why am I so upset about nothing? It continued for quite some time.

Then it occurred to me: Ah, it's demons of discord! Demons love to cause division and provoke disharmony. So I repeated this deliverance prayer for about fifteen minutes: *Causa discordiae, vade! Causa discordiae, vade!* (Demons of discord, depart.) It suddenly stopped, and a feeling of harmony returned, confirming my discernment of a demonic influence.

The next day, I checked with two other team members, and they had also experienced unexplained, unnatural discord around the same time. Satan continues to attack our team in a variety of ways, particularly when we are involved with an intense case. One of the first signs of a demonic influence is discord. We counter it with prayer and then a team meeting. This is the best antidote to demonic discord: prayer and communication.

We are trained to recognize Satan's influence and then to counteract it. I am certain that many, many families, communities, and organizations are subject to the same powerful demonic discord. But they may not realize where it is coming from and may fall victim to its strife and discord.

There is also no doubt in my mind that the demons of discord are now running rife in this country. The same antidote applies: prayer and open communication. It is clear that God is protecting our deliverance team as we continue to do our best to do His will. If families, communities, and nations willingly give themselves over to doing God's will and respond to discord with prayer and communication, they, too, will be protected.

"All Hell Broke Loose"—Literally!

We received a frantic call from a man in Indiana who was a nonpracticing Baptist. His wife was not a believer. They had two children. They recently inherited their house from relatives. The man who previously lived in the house was known to have molested minors and was involved in the occult. He died in April, and this family moved in around June. Shortly after they moved in, "all hell broke loose"—literally.

The family saw dark, shadowy figures. There were radical temperature drops in isolated places in the house, such as from 70 degrees to 30 degrees. The dog barked uncontrollably. The children heard a "voice" from the basement calling to them.

They often heard strange noises and banging. At night, a "presence" got on the father's chest and pinned him down. He couldn't move and could barely breathe. When this happened, he commanded out loud, "In the name of Jesus, get off me!" He did this three times, and it stopped.

The family continued to hear loud bangs, a voice say, "Hey," and whistling. They also experienced what sounded like someone jumping on the floor above, shaking objects in the room. The daughter felt something touch her leg and she saw a shadowy figure. Kitchen drawers slammed shut. They heard sounds like someone walking around. The wife felt a breeze of air while in the shower, and it felt as if something was in the shower with her. It all sounded like a real-life horror movie.

The first priest they contacted seemed skeptical. He asked them if they had mice. They were obviously upset by this and said to me, "These things are very real, very scary, and very nasty. I feel like until someone experiences what we are experiencing, they won't understand what we're going through and how all of this is affecting everything in our lives." The entire family was terrified and were sleeping together in the same bedroom at night.

The family contacted us. After our initial investigation, we realized that this was indeed an emergency that could destroy the family and their emotional health. So I immediately contacted the Catholic priest in the nearby parish. He said he was about to go on vacation the next day. I explained the situation to him. He dropped everything and exorcised the house that evening. God bless him!

A few days later, I contacted the father of the family. I asked, "How is it?" He responded, "I would say things are better because before things were really bad. The sounds of walking on the floor and sounds of banging and tapping have returned. But it is not as bad."

After the priest returned from vacation, I asked him to exorcise the house a second time, which he did. It has been over a year now, and all continues to be quiet in the house. The demonic infestation is apparently gone.

There was no doubt that the house was infested. First, there was a clear reason for the presence of demons. The previous owner had molested minors and practiced the occult — two major demonic doorways. The new owners were basically sane people, and the wife didn't even believe in such stuff (until it started happening to her). The reported symptoms were classic signs of a demonic infestation. And the members of the family were so truly terrified that they slept in the same room.

Happily, there was a generous priest nearby who assisted. Also, it was great that it took only two sessions. With deeply entrenched demonic presences, it can take many more.

Not surprisingly, that family now sits in the front pew of their church on Sundays. The father told me, "We have grown a really strong bond with the pastor and other church members." He added, "We have thanked God and continue to thank God for the blessings He has given us."

Theological Reflection

In a Demonic Emergency, Call a Priest!

Recently, our team has had a number of non-Catholics, including Jewish and Muslim folks, come to us for help. We are very glad to help, and in a moment of crisis we don't push the idea of becoming Catholic. Rather, we respect the religious choices of their consciences.

Nevertheless, I wonder: Why do they come to us? They tell me it is commonly known that if you have problems with demons, you call a Catholic priest.

Ironically, most priests do not receive any formal training in deliverance. The subject is almost universally ignored in the seminary. Yet a lot of people know that when you are harassed by demons, you need a priest.

The reason is simple. In Luke 9:1, we read, "Jesus summoned the Twelve and gave them power and authority over all demons." While all Christians, by virtue of their Baptism, can invoke the holy name of Jesus and pray to God that demons be cast out, Jesus gave His twelve apostles unique authority to do so. This authority has been passed down in an unbroken line to the bishops and priests of today.

We respect the religious choices of those who come to us. But wouldn't it make sense for them to look more deeply into the incredible spiritual realities of the Catholic Church? When a priest begins to pray the ancient prayers of the Church over the demons, they scream in agony. They hate us because when we pray, it is Christ Himself in His Church who is praying. And the "gates of hell will not prevail against it" (see Matt. 16:18).

It may be that, through such intense and powerful encounters, God is calling the afflicted people to a personal relationship with Jesus, and perhaps in the Church that He founded.

Exorcist Diary 91

She Who Crushes the Serpent

"Lucy" is possessed and being tortured nightly by the demons. They taunt her, mark her body with scratches and burns, claim that they own her, and often twist her injured leg, which is excruciating for her. Demons are merciless and relentless.

After a number of intense exorcism sessions, the demons were weakening. It seemed to me that they just might be weak enough to be compelled by the power of Jesus to reveal their names. Having their demonic names gives additional power to cast them out and suggests that the time of their exit is approaching.

So I demanded again and again: *"Dicas mihi nomen tuum"* (Tell me your name). This line is a direct quote from the traditional Rite of Exorcism. The demon resisted mightily. Finally, with great reluctance, it gave up its name: Abyzou.

I looked it up. Several sources concur: Abyzou (also spelled Abizou, Obizu, Obizuth, Obyzouth, and Byzou) is the name of a "female" demon in the Near East blamed for miscarriages and infant mortality.[50]

---

[50] Demons do not have physical bodies or gender, so it is technically not a male or female.

It made perfect sense. Sadly, Lucy had had an abortion. She sincerely repented, went to Confession, and remained very contrite. While any and all sins are forgiven in the sacrament, this does not mean that associated demons are immediately cast out. Often, a time of purgation is necessary. Given the gravity of the sin and the resulting tragic death of the child, it was going to be a fight to cast out this demon.

Abyzou taunted Lucy for having had an abortion. The demon told her she could never be forgiven. It played on her deep sense of guilt and attempted to drag her into the darkness of hopelessness and despair. This is typical demonic behavior. Demons not only tempt you to commit sin, but, if you do sin, they taunt you and shame you for doing so. We assured Lucy that her sin was truly forgiven and said a prayer for her baby. Lucy may also need post-abortion counseling or to work with post-abortion healing groups.

In the midst of the session, one of the exorcists was inspired to hold up an icon of Our Lady of Guadalupe. The demon went into a huge convulsion. So, repeatedly we invoked Our Lady under this title, and the demon convulsed every time the icon was held up.

The effectiveness of this holy image is no accident. The icon of Our Lady of Guadalupe reveals Mary as a pregnant woman, and she is often invoked under this title for unborn children. Moreover, under her feet is a symbol of the moon and darkness, a reference to the devil. Juan Diego, upon whose tilma the image appeared, referred to her in his native language as *Te Coatlazopeuh*—"she who crushes the serpent."

Abortion is a grievous sin. But Lucy and others should know that there is a divine source of healing and peace. We have a tremendous advocate in Our Lady of Guadalupe, who treads upon Abyzou and brings God's healing.

Our Lady of Guadalupe, mystical rose, pray for us.

Exorcist Diary 92

Satan's Ploy

I remember remarking to a fellow exorcist that, as a psychologist, I felt a special closeness to those suffering from mental problems. About ten days later, a young woman came in requesting an exorcism. She explained that she had a mental illness. She was more than attractive and dressed in a *very* provocative way. I had an immediate insight (likely from my guardian angel) into Satan's ploy. I thought, "Nice try, Lucifer." I suggested she continue to work with her mental health counselor.

Sadly, there have been cases in which exorcists, some well known, have left the priesthood in the course of their ministry. I was recently asked why. In two of the cases, the exorcists had become sexually involved with people who came to them for assistance.

There are two primary goals for Satan in every case of possession. The second goal is to keep the afflicted person from being liberated. Satan will fight viciously to keep this from happening. But his first goal is to destroy the vocation of the priest and the team's ministry. This would not only stop this exorcism; it would eventually stop all their exorcisms.

Satan will attempt to divide the team, causing division among team members. He will likely get inside team members' heads and subject them to demonic obsessions, self-doubt, guilt, and recriminations. And he will tempt the exorcists directly.

It is for these reasons that we put in place strong safeguards. To reduce conflict and division, team members regularly communicate honestly and openly. We make use of strong binding prayers and prayers of protection with every session. We also have firm boundaries: every exorcism session has several people in the room, including another woman if the afflicted person is a female.

Also, it helps to have a chief exorcist who is an older priest present—like me; I'm over seventy! It is not a ministry for a newly ordained priest, unless he works under direct supervision. Satan is crafty and knows our weaknesses. It takes a team approach to keep everyone safe, and it helps to have our guardian angels always watching our backs.

Exorcist Diary 93

Demons of Despair

When "Gary" came in for his session, you could cut the feeling of despair around him with a knife, it was so palpable. He had always struggled a bit with hopelessness, but this time it was incredibly strong. A thought went through my head: "Don't try to talk him out of it; *pray* him out of it." So we immediately went into an intense exorcism session. At the end of it, the despair was gone, and he was back to his peaceful self.

As a psychologist, I typically endeavor to have people get in touch with their feelings and to "own" them. If they don't, they are liable to "stuff" their emotions, and then those emotions come out "sideways," in all sorts of dysfunctional ways, such as alcohol abuse, drugs, sex, porn, nasty behavior, and more. This is particularly true of what people call "negative" emotions, such as anger, hurt, resentment, and darker emotions such as despair. We humans need to learn to manage these more difficult emotions.

Now, I have to make an adjustment in my thinking. Most of the time, what I have said is true. But there are times when people's emotions don't come from their psyche; they come from the bowels of Hell. Or more likely, the person may feel a *little* of these negative emotions, and then Satan *exaggerates* them into an overwhelming crisis.

This only makes sense. When demons are present, they infect you with their evil psyche. They are immersed in narcissism, fear, paranoia, anger, and, yes, despair. It is for good reason that Dante's *Inferno* has inscribed over the gates of Hell, "Abandon all hope, ye who enter here." Having definitively rejected God, demons and the damned have forever rejected the true source of all hope.

There are many things that happen in the course of an exorcism, and the transformation from despair to hope is one of them. I have often seen the light of God's hope shine once again in the faces of the afflicted, who sometimes began in the mire of a demonic despair.

When grappling with dark feelings of despair, oftentimes people need a psychologist. But there are times when only an exorcist will do.

Exorcist Diary 94

Wounded in Spiritual Combat

It was a particularly ugly session. After months of exorcism sessions, I now had the demon leader's name. I moved in close to the possessed, about two feet away, and stared the demons in the eye. The demons were fully manifested. Using the leader's name, I commanded them, in the name of Jesus, to leave.

They didn't budge.

These demons were not yet weak enough to be cast out and had plenty of fight left in them. In a gravelly voice, they mocked and taunted me. I could hear and feel the evil. They were disgusting and full of filth. I tried not to listen.

I try not to make this a personal fight. I hide behind Jesus and do everything in His name. It is He who is the exorcist. But it's a bit difficult being only twenty-four inches away from the demons who are in a full rage. The demons took all this very personally, as they always do, and focused their seething violence on me.

Finally, it was time to end the session. The team members and the afflicted person were all tired. Together we said prayers of thanksgiving. At the beginning of the session, I had faithfully said prayers of protection. Now, at the closing, I said the full cleansing prayers.

But when it all ended, I wasn't feeling quite right. I tried relaxing, eating dinner, and moving on. Nothing helped. I tried to ride it out, but after an hour or so, I wasn't any better. In fact, I felt somewhat disabled.

I was eventually able to identify the feeling. I felt as if I had been stabbed by a poisoned blade. I was spiritually wounded. The poison was there, and it would not go away. It was infecting my entire system.

Apparently, for some reason, the demons were able to break through the usual protection and "stab" me with their poison. Perhaps I had gotten too close. Regardless, I was wounded with an otherworldly poison.

There was only one solution for this. I went into the chapel and asked my Mother for help. It seemed to me that she looked at me with kindness and gently chided me for waiting so long to come to her. She quickly expelled the poison. I was then fine, although I needed to rest a bit.

I don't know how the demons were able to get through. It reminds me of what one of my military instructors said. While training us in knife fighting, he gave us the following admonition: "In a knife fight, you are going to get cut."

In a close fight with demons, I have to expect to get "cut" occasionally. But I learned my lesson. Next time, my first stop will be the chapel and the healing touch of Our Lady.

Exorcist Diary 95

"She Will Come"

Jason's possession (see entry 71) was one of the most difficult we have faced, perhaps as difficult as any exorcist can face. He was possessed by hundreds of demons, with Satan himself personally leading them. But the more difficult the case, the stronger the graces God gives. In this case, I knew that we would need the very best God could send.

We were coming close to the end, after countless hours of ugly and painful sessions. The demons were getting weaker and were now more obedient, much to their dismay. I commanded them, in the name of Jesus, to tell us, "When will you leave, and by what means?" The demons reluctantly responded with a date two weeks hence and said, "She will come."

Everyone in the room knew who "she" was. The demons would not say the name of the Mother of God. Her name, like that of her Son, is itself holy.

The day finally came, and the moment approached. The room grew silent, and Jason said, "She is here." As the Virgin quietly moved closer, the demons began to thrash wildly. She said nothing, but the radiant light of Christ shining through the humble handmaid of God was overpowering.

Satan himself screamed. After screaming and thrashing several times, the prince of darkness left. It was over.

Now I ask all of the possessed to consecrate themselves to the Mother of God as part of the healing process. We ask Mary not only to cast out the demons but to protect the afflicted persons for the rest of their lives, until she welcomes them into the Kingdom.

The gates of Hell will not prevail against the Church or against her Mother.

Theological Reflection

The Faith Affirmed

One of the great graces of this deliverance ministry is experiencing firsthand the truths of our Faith. In some way, directly or indirectly, exorcisms regularly affirm what our Faith teaches.

To begin with, the divine order is clear. There is one God, whom the demons hate. Satan is powerful but still merely a creature on a short leash. There are good angels assisting us and evil demons bent solely on controlling and destruction. The Blessed Virgin is our most powerful intercessor. These fundamental truths are part of the landscape of every session.

The Communion of Saints? We regularly experience the power of the saints and their direct assistance. The authority of the Church? When I invoke the "keys of St. Peter," there is sometimes a shudder among the possessing demons. The importance of the sacraments? The first stop in the healing process is going to Confession. Moreover, the possessed person often has great problems going to Mass, receiving the Eucharist, or praying in Eucharistic adoration: The demons hate it! Their strong aversion to the Eucharist is a testament to the Real Presence of Christ.

The ordained priesthood? The presence of a priest is a demon's nightmare. They hate us and the power of Christ that we wield. Sacramentals? The entire Rite of

Exorcism is a powerful sacramental, and we regularly use a crucifix, holy water, exorcised oil, relics of the saints, and other holy objects. Time and again, we witness the effect that these instruments of God's holiness has over the demons.

The demons are dedicated to destroying all that God has ordained. But their lives and actions actually give glory to God and help to accomplish His holy will. For example, instead of destroying our faith, the action of the demons in these cases affirms and strengthens our faith, as it has for so many of the energumens and their families.

I thank God for this ministry and His powerful graces working through it all.

Concluding Comments

I hope that these diary entries have given you insights into the deliverance ministry and the daily experiences of an exorcist.

I have exaggerated nothing. I have made up nothing. I do not say that my reflections are *de fide*. I claim no special authority. Rather, I refer all to the teachings of the Catholic Church for an authentic understanding of the message of Jesus. They are simply my experiences as I interpret them, and they are subject to my own errors in perception and understanding.

No doubt some exorcists will disagree on some of the points I have made. No problem. I expect some to disagree on certain points. But in conversation with other exorcists, I find that our experiences are surprisingly similar. This is a confirmation for us of these spiritual realities.

For too long, this ministry has been relegated either to ancient history, superstition, or to the remnants of prescientific thinking. Modern science is important, but science is unable to plumb deeper spiritual realities.

There have been more than a few cases in which the medical and psychological sciences have proven unable to help, and the prayers of the Church dissipated the problem rather quickly. Most of the time, however, I find that the psychological sciences and our spiritual ministry work well together and complement each other. I often witness the necessity of working on both levels for any real resolution to an afflicted person's suffering.

I have been a bit surprised in recent times by those who would say that exorcisms were not an integral part of the ministry of Jesus and thus are not an integral part of today's Church. To reject the reality of Satan and his direct activity in people's lives is to relegate Sacred Scripture to a theologically inaccurate anachronism. If one begins to face the existence of evil head-on, then one has to face the stark and uncomfortable truths of the full teachings of Jesus.

Did Jesus really face Satan in the desert? Did Jesus really mean to say that in Hell there is an eternity of "wailing and grinding of teeth" (Matt. 13:42)? It is interesting how people can read the Gospels over a lifetime and psychologically deny some of these awful truths. It is as if people have become accustomed to mentally blocking out these important, although ugly, realities.

Perhaps the reflections in this diary are, at times, unsettling. Maybe they should be. The gospel itself should not be so comfortable that we are completely at ease with it.

For example, I cannot fathom an eternity in Hell, but Jesus says it is real. Also, I have difficulty accepting the notion of spiritual beings completely given over to evil, and yet Satan and his demons exist. When I stand in the same room and face them, their raging murderous evil is very real and very disturbing. Facing evil should be disturbing.

But it is my hope that you will walk away from these diary reflections with the same Spirit that flows through our exorcism team. We are a happy group. We enjoy dinners together, many laughs, and a pervasive joy in the spiritual life and in our grace-filled ministry.

After a day of facing evil, enduring demonic attacks, and suffering with the souls under our care, we rest secure in the knowledge that evil has been definitively defeated in Christ. As the day ends, I sprinkle holy water around my room, commend myself to the protection of the Blessed Virgin, and sleep soundly in the arms of our Mother.

St. Michael Center for Spiritual Renewal (www.catholic-exorcism.org) has an app, Catholic Exorcism. This free app, as well as the website, provides many important deliverance and exorcism prayers in English and Spanish for laity, priests, and exorcists. Both the website and the app have many other resources, such as Church documents on the deliverance ministry and Msgr. Rossetti's very popular blog.

About the Author

Msgr. Stephen J. Rossetti, Ph.D., is the President of the St. Michael Center for Spiritual Renewal and a research associate professor at the Catholic University of America in Washington, D.C. A licensed psychologist and the author of several books, Msgr. Rossetti has participated in hundreds of exorcisms. During his journey to priesthood, he experienced a spiritual episode in which, "in two seconds I learned 80 percent of what an exorcist needs to know."

Sophia Institute

Sophia Institute is a nonprofit institution that seeks to nurture the spiritual, moral, and cultural life of souls and to spread the Gospel of Christ in conformity with the authentic teachings of the Roman Catholic Church.

Sophia Institute Press fulfills this mission by offering translations, reprints, and new publications that afford readers a rich source of the enduring wisdom of mankind.

Sophia Institute also operates the popular online resource CatholicExchange.com. *Catholic Exchange* provides world news from a Catholic perspective as well as daily devotionals and articles that will help readers to grow in holiness and live a life consistent with the teachings of the Church.

In 2013, Sophia Institute launched Sophia Institute for Teachers to renew and rebuild Catholic culture through service to Catholic education. With the goal of nurturing the spiritual, moral, and cultural life of souls, and an abiding respect for the role and work of teachers, we strive to provide materials and programs that are at once enlightening to the mind and ennobling to the heart; faithful and complete, as well as useful and practical.

Sophia Institute gratefully recognizes the Solidarity Association for preserving and encouraging the growth of our apostolate over the course of many years. Without their generous and timely support, this book would not be in your hands.

www.SophiaInstitute.com
www.CatholicExchange.com
www.SophiaInstituteforTeachers.org

Sophia Institute Press® is a registered trademark of Sophia Institute. Sophia Institute is a tax-exempt institution as defined by the Internal Revenue Code, Section 501(c)(3). Tax ID 22-2548708.